Creative Design
for Fashion and Embroidery

Creative Design
for Fashion and Embroidery

NORMAN W. PHILIPSON

Studio Vista
London

Acknowledgements

I would like to express my gratitude to the following: those intrepid adult students at Loughborough College of Art and Design, whose unbounded enthusiasm has made this book possible; all the students whose work is illustrated in this book; colleagues Lyn Nicol, Winifred Aldrich and Ann Shipside for their constructive comments; and my editor, Susannah Read, for her generous assistance in the creation of this book.

Photographs 73 and 74 are reproduced by courtesy of the Victoria and Albert Museum, London, and 83 by courtesy of the British Museum, London.

Studio Vista

An imprint of Cassell & Collier Macmillan Publishers Ltd,
35 Red Lion Square, London WC1R 4SG,
and at Sydney, Auckland, Toronto, Johannesburg,
an affiliate of Macmillan Inc., New York

Copyright © Norman W. Philipson 1976
First published in 1976

ISBN 0 289 70588 6

Designed by C. H. Paulin
Set in 11 on 12 pt Bembo
Filmset and printed in Great Britain by
BAS Printers Limited, Wallop, Hampshire

Contents

1 Introduction – **7**

2 Why Design? – **9**

3 Line – **15**

4 Shape and Form – **28**

5 Pattern – **37**

6 Texture – **43**

7 Colour – **51**

8 Design through Materials – **59**

9 Sources of Inspiration – **71**

10 Development of an Idea – **79**

11 Crticism – **91**

Some Further Reading – **94**

Index – **95**

1 Introduction

For a number of years I have been teaching design to adults. Although many professed to have no design ability, let alone the ability to draw, within a short space of time and much to their own surprise they were able to practise design in quite an imaginative manner.

Two very popular women's crafts, fashion (dressmaking) and embroidery, embrace some traditions which it is very hard to change, although for a number of years organizations interested in the development of these subjects have attempted to improve the state of affairs. These bodies have only touched the tip of the iceberg, slowly drawing attention to the need for design as well as technique.

One of the best ways of achieving this aim is to step back from familiar processes and materials and turn to very basic materials, such as paint, pencil and paper, to experience design in a simple, immediate manner. By doing this you will realize how limiting and shortsighted it is to view fashion and embroidery in isolation from one another and from other areas of design.

At the centre of the debate is a chicken and egg situation. Which comes first, or is more important, design or technique? Should you become proficient in the techniques of the subject and then discover the mysteries of design, or should you make a study of design first?

Look at another band of enthusiasts, photographers, who are equally concerned with design and technique. There are those whose interest is only in perfection of technique, in reducing the content and composition of the photograph to a series of clichés designed to show off the sophistication of their equipment. While there are others who put the organization of the visual idea first, using their technical skills to realize an imaginative visual image which will act as an eye-stopping communicator.

So with fashion and embroidery; the visual image is again the point of contact, a common enough assumption in professional design circles, but sadly overlooked by the amateur.

I have found that if the word design is mentioned, people usually feel it is something much too difficult to understand, let alone practise, or is some special gift from heaven which rests on the shoulders of a few chosen individuals. I would like to show that design need not be difficult to understand or to practise and that everyone has much more innate design ability than we give credit for. I will endeavour to illustrate how design occupies a central position in our lives and therefore a most important role in such crafts as fashion and embroidery.

2 *Why Design?*

Each day we make decisions which affect the appearance of our immediate visual environment. Many of these may seem quite unimportant, just jobs which have to be done.

Consider such activities as placing bedding plants in the garden, arranging furniture in a room, or setting a table for a meal. You may make some of the decisions they require unconsciously, for a similar situation will probably have arisen many times before. With the rush and bustle of everyday routine, there is often little time to reflect on the final effect or the stages which lead up to the completed scheme. Let us consider the second example, furniture in a room, in a little more detail. Why did you place a chair in a particular position? Did you unconsciously consider how the room is used, the shape and colour of the chair and how these factors relate to the overall decorative scheme? A professional designer would take all these points and others into consideration, taking care to achieve the right balance and effect. When you look at a designer's solution to a problem, you might be tempted to say, 'What a marvellous idea, how simple, how unusual, how effective. Why didn't I think of that?' But don't fall into the trap of assuming the designer created the arrangement in a blinding flash of inspiration. This is far from the truth, for the final effect was the sum total of very many small, perhaps insignificant, decisions sensitively welded into a coherent solution.

Design has achieved a greater measure of popular appeal during recent years. Many major exhibitions, such as Expo 67 in Montreal, have high-lighted the international appeal of design. The Olympic Games has become a forum for advanced design concepts, where architectural design and graphic design in posters, literature and international sign language systems provide competition to the real purpose of the event, that is competition on the track.

Manufacturers are conscious of good design as a selling point for their products and this is further reinforced when design is discussed as an important ingredient of living by magazines. Environment has become a popular cause, and it is now politically expedient to consider the visual form of our surroundings.

During the nineteenth century many traditional crafts, which contained a very strong natural design element, suffered through competition from machines. Natural links between the designer and the craftsman concerning suitability of material, proportion and shape were weakened and designers began to think more in terms of applied decoration. Industrialization caused towns to grow into cities at a furious pace, spawning, in the process, houses which were destined quickly to become slums whose inhabitants had little time or opportunity to improve or consider their surroundings. The factories

Latest Paris fashions from a
supplement to *Queen*, January 3
5

9

which produced the landscape of spoil tips and 'dark satanic mills' also produced far-reaching changes which have had a profound influence on present day society. One of these was the opportunity of education for all, and another, perhaps a mixed blessing, was to lay the foundations of our consumer-orientated society.

Nowadays we all have expectations of an increasing range of creature comforts. Advertising, a highly organized industry for well over a century, has convinced us of the need to possess the latest creations of manufacturers. The Great Exhibition of 1851 in London's Hyde Park presented a wealth of highly ornate products – from furniture, ceramics and fabrics to highly decorated, new industrial machinery. This rich array of merchandise was produced through the skill of many for the pleasure and use of only a small proportion of the population. At this time, before full automation, perfection in technique was important and workers were encouraged to see it as the supreme achievement. Rich, ornate clothes, using many yards of material, and complex, detailed stitchery, could only be realized through a skilled workforce toiling for long hours. If people were able to have any pride at all in their work it was in being able to perfect complex techniques. In most cases creativity was restricted by rigid convention, which precluded any experiment outside the traditional idiom, or was the preserve of a few individuals.

Education did very little to improve this situation. Industry needed a trained workforce, clerks with an adequate standard of reading, writing and arithmetic. Designers were required to be little more than skilled technicians, able to copy pattern to standards required by local industries. The emphasis at that particular time was on changing the country from a rural to an industrial state. We now realize that sights were set very low, to provide a crash education programme which catered for the needs of industry, but did an absolute minimum in terms of educating the individual.

Many practices which appeared in the early years of mass education exist today, even though social conditions and educational objectives have changed

2 Industrialization caused towns to expand enormously

completely. Some practices are regarded now as 'traditional' even though
their life has been comparatively short. Perhaps the greatest difficulty in
making progress today is to identify these traditions, which are often practised
by people who consider themselves enlightened.

Very many people today are still resistant to change, particularly, I have
noticed, those attending adult education classes. This is probably due to a fear
of the unknown; the caged bird doesn't want to leave the cage when it is
offered its freedom.

Some years ago, while living in Ghana, I visited a village whose inhabitants
specialized in wood carving (there were other villages specializing in weaving
and fabric printing). The village produced many traditional objects, one of
which was fertility dolls, called *akua'ba*, worn by a girl when she desired a
child. The basic form of the doll was traditional but it was surprising to see
the many variations of style. Some dolls were better designed than others, for
contrary to popular belief good and bad design can exist in more primitive
art forms and the same basic criteria for criticism, which we will be considering
later, hold good. In this case some of the carvers were giving the heads of the
dolls a European look instead of the classic features of an Ashanti girl. In other
words, they were getting their objectives mixed. Nevertheless, all the carvers
reached a basic level of accomplishment. As this activity was a way of life in
the village there was no question of taking a person's artistic ability into
account before he became a carver; such an idea would never be considered.

Education in an industrial society can remove people from a way of life
where they make full use of their natural abilities. I noticed many Ghanaian
university graduates were in the same position in this respect as people from
more industrialized nations. As a person grows older there is a falling off of
confidence in certain directions. A child, for instance, is quite happy to draw,
paint and use his imagination. As training becomes more advanced and
specialized, confidence in unpractised skills begins to decline, so that by the
time the child becomes an adult he or she is sure that certain basic abilities are
well beyond reach.

Is it possible for anyone to practise design, given the opportunity? I would quite unreservedly say yes. I have met many people who say they can't draw, paint or design, or express themselves another way by saying they have no imagination. Yet within a few weeks of receiving instruction aimed at identifying elements of design they are thinking through problems, painting pictures and creating designs, which illustrate quite a high degree of imagination and artistic skill. I have seen ample material to illustrate my point that there exists a large, untapped reservoir of these resources amongst both men and women. In most cases, especially among older adults, lack of confidence was bred by poor teaching methods. Even with younger people it could be due to insufficient encouragement by the teacher who has perhaps dropped the casual comment, 'You can't draw,' or simply never taken the trouble to select the pupil's work for any special comment or praise. As it was the teacher who made these comments, they were readily accepted. Many people who left school more than twenty years ago will still say, 'I can't draw, I was no good at school.' They have lost confidence in their ability to use a vital part of their basic skill.

So many people have been discouraged from expressing their emotions that to pick up a brush, mix paint and generally put marks on paper often demands from them enormous reserves of courage. The pastel drawing (5) and the flower painting (56) were studies created at home, with supervision, after only twelve weeks' experience of drawing and design. It will no doubt surprise you that both these women said they couldn't draw. Progress during this initial period was quite astounding, rather like water irrigating a desert which suddenly bursts into bloom, sprouting plants of all descriptions. Both these students had to make their own decisions not to resort to a formula or cliché, but to rely on reasoned judgement on selection of subject material, composition, selection and order of colour, shape and pattern within the drawing and painting. Quite a list of criteria, yet they were consciously and intuitively managed. When you are experiencing design, in the final analysis, the form of the end product matters least; the thought process involved offers greater stimulation and in the long term is more important.

At what point does this relate to fashion and embroidery? For most people the connection between painting and fashion is rather remote, while the link with embroidery is much easier to understand. Fashion and embroidery are traditionally recognized as women's crafts and practised in the home. Yet embroidery is a creative, expressive medium making intellectual demands similar to those of painting and sculpting. Fashion is also creative on at least two levels: that of the designer projecting an image of women and that of the woman wearing clothes made or selected by herself.

Possibly the greatest danger is to see these subjects in isolation. In order to make this point a little clearer, let us consider a much wider range of activities which tend to be placed in their own separate compartments: architecture, landscape gardening, pottery, furniture making, jewelry and advertising. These activities do have a common denominator, but let us leave that aside for the moment. Look at each one to decide if it is possible to divide the subject to fit it under two headings, visual element and method. It should be possible without any great difficulty to make a division in this way. A much more demanding problem would be to determine the relative importance of visual element and method. At a first glance you might say the two categories were equally important, but this is not necessarily so.

4 Fertility doll, 30 cm (1 inches) high, from Ghana

Pastel drawing of pansies,
made after less than twelve
weeks' study

Perhaps more than at any other time the mass of the population, as opposed to the few in earlier periods of our history, are vitally aware of the value of our environment. Coal tips are now flattened and planted with trees and grass to blend with their surroundings, while gravel pits become boating lakes and nature trails. Factory sites are landscaped, wherever possible, to allow buildings to enhance rather than diminish the quality of working conditions.

The methods or techniques of the subjects on my list vary considerably and there might be one or two areas where techniques overlap. So where is this common denominator? Well, I would say it is in the visual element. We all have the ability to *see* our environment. Whether we do is another matter!

A parallel can be drawn with another of our senses, hearing. A musician is more likely to be able to differentiate between one note and another than someone who hasn't had the benefit of his training and experience. Few people would dispute this. Unfortunately, when we consider the visual world each person considers himself an expert, implying that we have all been using our eyes since we were born. People just don't realize how selective we can be when we see and hear. We have a tremendous ability to shut out sounds and images we don't immediately require; if we couldn't, life would be unbearable. For example, a person working in a noisy factory can shut out sound, learning to live with it by talking above the level of noise; in dismal, depressing surroundings he would try to dismiss the more unpleasant aspects from his vision. Today many people who live in congested cities are subjected to noise and far from ideal surroundings. This encourages experience of sound and vision to contract. In the process the faculty for critical judgement becomes limited.

Although the visual element can be considered a common denominator to the activities listed, how can it be defined? Colour, shape, form, pattern and texture cover the major groupings of the elements of our visual world. Most people are vaguely aware of these elements; they see them every day but understanding their place, function and relationship remains an unsolved mystery.

Not so the professional; through either training or experience, he has learnt to recognize these as his most important tools to be used with care and imagination. A few years ago a number of the world's leading graphic designers, representing many countries, met to discuss, among other topics, the training of designers in universities and colleges. They agreed unanimously that the most important aspect was the development of visual awareness. There were a number of interpretations of this concept, some more elaborate than others. But to everyone present it meant more than awareness of your environment; it involved the ability to choose, to express your feelings and to examine problems in a more intuitive manner, in order to produce solutions which do not necessarily fit into traditional patterns.

Quite a demanding list, but would these criteria apply to anyone wishing to expand their understanding and feeling for design in fashion and embroidery? You might say at this moment, 'I'm only doing this for pleasure; I'm not a professional; I don't need this much experience'. However, it's difficult to ask for less; after all, these are only avenues to be explored as part of a continuous process, building experience on experience. Take heart, the demands of design look far more daunting on paper than they are in practice.

Another much more simple way of looking at this activity is to be openminded and determined always to broaden your experience. The least profitable way of doing this is through theory alone, therefore where possible I would like to present you with a series of practical experiments which, if approached as I suggest, should provide the kind of experience I have been discussing in this chapter.

The first experiments will be quite simple and will not require so-called artistic ability, or previous drawing experience, but rather an interest in solving problems as they arise. I will try to propel you along a path, providing you with a particular experience, which at times will require a certain amount of staying power. As a result of these experiences I hope you will discover a greater range of opportunities for creating imaginative design in fashion and embroidery, and see how these ideas can relate to other aspects of life.

I will break these elements of design into the following components: line, shape and form, pattern, texture, and colour. Later I will show how these relate to developing ideas, and provide criteria for discussing good and bad design.

3 *Line*

Line is an element which appears again and again in design, sometimes on its own and sometimes in conjunction with other elements, such as shape. In both fashion and embroidery it plays a fundamental role: in stitchery and as pattern and pleats or folds on fabric. I would like you to examine line from many different viewpoints in order to discover the tremendous range of possibilities which stem from a single theme.

We are all aware of line in some form or another. Examples will come to mind by looking around a room, or considering lingering images within your past experience. You might remember early childhood visions: the long, looping lines of power cables as they stride across the countryside, the straight lines and precise curves of railway tracks, the meandering line formed by a stream or river, or repeated vertical lines formed by tree trunks in a pine forest.

Were you to walk through the countryside or town, observing and listing as many kinds of line as possible, you would soon have made a long list. This could no doubt be broken down into a number of categories, which become more sharply defined if they are arranged to contrast with one another to bring out their special qualities. There are straight and curved, smooth and ragged, jagged and billowing, wavy and meandering lines; you can no doubt think of many more. In a short space of time you will realize that a line may possess more than one of these qualities, which adds many new permutations for consideration.

Another method of classifying line is through scale. You can either contrast one line with another, saying this is a thick line while that is a thin one, or you can relate lines to human scale. Did you, as a child, run through long grass, imagining it to be a jungle in which to hide? Perhaps when you look at the grass now you think it isn't that tall after all, or else it has shrunk! In each case you have been relating the size of the grass to the size of the person. Another factor to consider is the distance of the viewer from the object. A blade of grass a few inches from your nose looks massive, but when viewed from a normal standing position it is quite small. When you look at the ground from an upstairs window you see it from an even higher position. Perhaps it is only in more extreme circumstances, such as when looking down from an aircraft, a church tower, or tall building, that we see familiar images, such as cars and people, in a new perspective.

Normally our eyes, acting on our subconscious, observe these factors, and act on them only when required. Through design we find we become consciously aware of this visual information. It is not unusual to hear a person say, 'I walked along the road this morning and found myself seeing things with new eyes. I saw the pattern of lines formed by the branches of trees . . .' This

information will, no doubt, take its place in that person's memory to be used or drawn upon at some time in the future to form a valuable link in a design.

The best way of reaching this stage of awareness is to work through some practical experiments. We can learn much more about line if we begin to look at one or two basic forms, such as straight and curved lines.

Let us consider straight lines first. Take a large sheet of white paper, as a background on which you can place a number of thin strips of black paper. As a variation on this theme you can use a black background and place a number of white strips of paper on it; this can be very effective. The strips, whether white or black, should all be the same width, about 6 mm ($\frac{1}{4}$ inch) wide and about 23 cm (9 inches) long. Through this project I would like you to discover how many different arrangements you can make using parallel lines.

First, arrange a number of black paper strips parallel to the top of the paper, equidistant to one another. Take another set, arrange these first of all in the same way, but do not glue them down. Now examine the white spaces between the lines; these we could call the negative image. Still keeping the lines parallel, concentrate on the negative image lines, endeavouring to create different line widths and develop an arrangement which is visually satisfying. In other words you are developing the design by looking at the spaces formed between the lines, rather than at the black lines themselves. You might have come to this conclusion yourself, seeing there is a fundamental relationship between the line and the surface on which it is placed. If you hadn't noticed, see if this is so in the arrangements you have completed.

Try a number of these arrangements on the rest of the paper; don't be in a rush to stick paper down, but try a number of different solutions. They will probably get better all the time. See if you can force the viewer to look at one region of the layout more than any other by creating a point of maximum interest. It is possible to make people look at a design in a certain way. You create a subtle pattern of viewing which is related to the position of the focal point so that the eye scans this area first, moves on to progressively less important zones before being dragged back to the starting point, to begin the process all over again. This might appear far-fetched – and it is a little over-simplified –

Power cable lines – a good ample of line in our vironment

8 Straight lines equidistant to one another

9 Keeping the lines parallel, manipulate the negative line images to develop an arrangement which is visually satisfying

10 Develop the ideas in **9** using lines which are no longer parallel. Where is the focal point of this arrangement?

but to evaluate its merits, see if other people look at the arrangements in the way you intend.

Another method of considering this phenomenon is to think of the focal point as the area of maximum tension within the design. In many ways this is a very sound approach, which allows designs to develop with a crisp, vibrant outlook. It suggests this point is critical, as indeed it is; the whole composition is highly tuned, balanced on a knife edge. Should the arrangement be even slightly altered, this moment is lost and the cohesion has gone. It might be replaced by an arrangement that is either better or worse, but it will never be the same.

What happens to straight lines when they appear on a surface which is no longer flat? This is an important question which has a particular relevance to fabrics and the manner in which they are used. Many fabric designs are composed of stripes; these become much more effective as soon as the natural folds of cloth are introduced. Pleating can change the character of a basic design; pleats can be of differing proportions and so once more the original stripe design appears to change. Lines also serve as a means of illustrating the contour of a surface, showing, for example, the position and size of folds without resort to highlight and shadow.

The only way of discovering more about the way line may be used on a curved surface is to experiment. You will find using simple materials, such as paper, much the best way of doing this. They are much more manageable than fabrics at this stage. In fact, people usually get much better results when they have to use materials which are alien to them, or use commonplace materials in quite a new way. Bearing this in mind I would like you to try gluing strips of paper onto a surface which will later be curved. Afterwards, try gluing strips of paper onto cylinders, this time pleating, folding or curving

11 A further projection of movement expressed through straight lines

the strips. You can also try out a series of small experiments on a flat, contrasting background. The illustrations on this page show a few ways in which these experiments might proceed.

Try to work in a controlled manner, taking a relatively simple starting point. As soon as you have a reasonable idea stick it down, using a quick-setting glue. Perhaps while you were sticking it down you began to think of modifying your idea, so do just that by making a 'mark 2' version, which can in turn be glued down. Before very long you will have a number of quite different solutions which will have grown from only two or three themes.

The mistake many people make is to try to be too original, feeling that each idea must be quite different from the previous one. Really, all you are doing is putting thoughts onto paper and allowing them to develop just as much through manipulating materials as through thinking hard about them. This is a concept to which we will return on many occasions.

Curved lines can present quite different effects to those created by straight lines. Your experiments with curved, folded and pleated lines will have opened up some new characteristics as well. Once again it is possible to understand more about curved lines through experiment than by reading a large amount of theory first. I would like you to form some of your own conclusions rather than simply accepting my observations. Use a large sheet of paper once more as the background. Cut out of thin card a template shape formed from part of the circumference of a circle. The circular part of the template will provide a constant curved line, which will form the basis of this exercise. Using a soft pencil and your template, draw a series of lines on the paper. Work quickly and impulsively, avoid completing the design area by area and try to develop the design as a whole unit, by working first in one area and then another. Step back from the work frequently so as to see the design from a different viewpoint. The diagram shows the starting point while the illustration shows a possible result; yours could appear quite different.

As you work through the exercise, watch the many changes which take place when many similar curved lines are repeated. Sometimes they form structures, while on other occasions they create pattern. Try to make some areas more dense than others in order to create a centre of interest. This region could be either more or less dense than the rest of the design, and its position also presents an interesting problem. Should it be near the top or bottom, in the centre or slightly off-centre? It's up to you to make the decision, bearing in mind the points which were raised when we were examining straight lines.

The mistake most people make is to stop too soon; to get a worthwhile effect you will have to draw many lines, allowing the overall design to present a dark grey appearance through sheer density of line. When you have completed the design, pin it to a wall, stand as far back as possible and take a contemplative look at the final result. You might be pleasantly surprised to notice the illusion of depth in the design. Allow your eyes to drift away from the centre of interest and back again, observing the structures and patterns which have formed. In many ways it is a similar sensation to that experienced when lying in bed seeing patterns formed by sunlight dissolve and re-form on the walls or curtains. If you have time to try another version, using the same template, see if you can arrive at a different, perhaps better result.

It is interesting to note curved lines in our surroundings: curved lines formed

12 What happens to straight lines when they are placed on curved surfaces? Try gluing strips of paper onto cylinders b pleating, cutting, folding or curving the strips

12

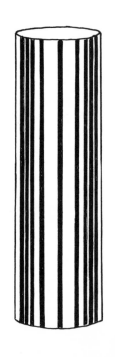

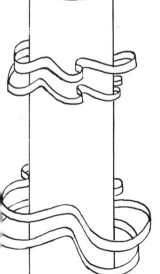

12

13 What happens to straight lines when they appear on a surface which is no longer flat? A loosely folded striped fabric shows how the shape and direction of the stripes describe the nature of the surface.

by branches of a willow tree, bubbles formed by detergent, the curves formed by cobblestones, or the pattern of granite paving blocks. There are many examples to choose from; look out for them, and notice the infinite variety of effect in curved line.

We so often think of line in a two-dimensional context, that is a line on a surface, that we forget another aspect, which is line in space. I have earlier drawn your attention to power cables, but there is a much lowlier example, the household washing line. Notice how this has an effect on its immediate surroundings. It does much more than join one post to another; it begins to identify space and makes you much more aware of the space surrounding the line. The branches of a willow tree when the leaves have fallen provide a good example of this effect. Each branch is piercing space, each one adding to the mass of the whole, by modifying space within the total area occupied by the tree. The tree occupies this space as if it were a solid mass, but of course it isn't.

With each of these probes I am trying to make you more aware of your surroundings, trying to help you both to see and feel more. Space and line in space is a combination which you must try to feel as well as see. To explore this further, make simple line structures from balsa wood, or thick copper wire, which allow interesting comparisons to be drawn between line in space and the two-dimensional quality of the shadow of the structure.

Although later we will be examining both pattern and texture, at this stage it is interesting to look at the way in which line might move into these areas. A very straightforward way is to make a printing block by gluing a piece of string onto a small block of wood. Poster paint can be used as the printing ink; apply it to the printing surface with a brush. If the surface area of the printing block is not too large, hand pressure will be quite sufficient to give a clean, even print. You may have some difficulty at the outset in finding the right

consistency and quantity of paint required to make the print but a short period of experiment will soon sort out this problem.

Some people start by making a self-conscious arrangement of the string on the block; often random placing onto the glued surface of the wood is much better. There are many different effects which can be achieved with the block, by overprinting images in many ways, sometimes relating the prints to a vertical or horizontal axis, or printing the design in a formal manner. On other occasions a more random approach might be more appropriate. See if the prints suggest ideas to you, rather than imposing a series of pre-considered constraints on the block. Try to work through the principle, 'I wonder what will happen if . . .?' In this way you are exploring and breaking new ground.

It is easy to be lulled into complacency by the first flush of success. After all, it is something quite different, a new experience, the results of which can be most exciting. I often feel that it is at this point the real work begins; unfortunately for some people this is where experiment stops. Gaining new experience can be a painful business. An athlete if she is going to improve her performance, has to train, push herself to the limit of her endurance, in order to jump higher than before, or run a distance in a shorter time. So it is with design. Of course you don't have to do physical exercises, but you do have to work hard to get over the first hurdle, which represents the previous limit of your experience. Most people can do this, for it is more within their capabilities than they realize.

Images obtained through this simple process can increase your sensitivity towards much freer forms of design, providing starting points for both embroidery and certain aspects of fashion. An obvious relationship is to machine embroidery, although you must not always assume a literal translation of an idea into these subjects is required; often the transitional stage will be much more subtle, providing oblique forms of inspiration to some aspect of design. You can perhaps prove this point yourself if you ask a number of people to look at some of your design sheets, for you will find they will wish to interpret them in different ways.

No doubt by now you are bubbling over with ideas on what is possible with line, having thought about this aspect of design. You have seen what can happen to curved and straight lines when they are used singly or built up to provide a mass. The methods used in the last exercise, where ideas were allowed to develop from a single theme, illustrate how minor changes of structure can provide quite different conclusions. As a final stage of this sequence, using brush and paint or pastels try to create as many different kinds of line as possible. It is useful to try to imagine these lines having emotive qualities; they might be, for example, aggressive, weak, slippery or fluffy.

This kind of work should be approached in a relaxed manner, allowing the images created by words to have maximum effect. Sensations are soon triggered off and provide a path for your exploration to follow. So much of what we have to do must come from within ourselves, with as much feeling and sympathy as we might require when listening to music. The opposite of this is a cold, mechanical outlook which usually leads to mechanical results.

So far we have been concerned with creating and looking at images and in many cases gradually modifying their structure through a process which was both intuitive and considered. Ideas have developed from marks on paper, or abstract thoughts. Line has become a familiar and much expanded concept.

We can now direct our attention to our surroundings, to see how many familiar forms are influenced by line, through either their outward appearance or structure. Earlier we discussed grass and its relationship to human scale. Let

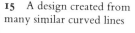

15 A design created from many similar curved lines

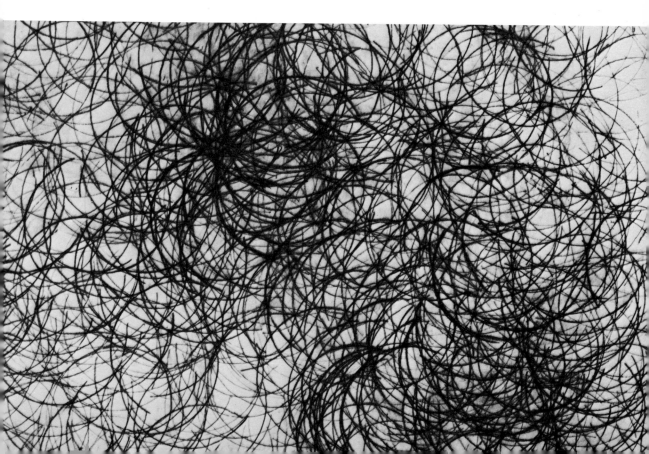

us now look at this plant from a different viewpoint. Examine a tuft of grass very closely and you will find it is composed of line in its total mass and structure. Notice how various structural points are formed, how line can be used to describe the appearance of the leaves. The roots of the plant continue the sequence; the fine, fibrous roots provide a line with quite a different character to the longer parallel lines above the ground. Thicker roots are as different again, depending very much on the species of grass you are looking at. Individual stems and leaves present rhythmic patterns between one another while also relating spatially. Different methods can be used to observe this; perhaps the easiest way is to look at the spaces between the stems and leaves, noticing the shapes these areas make. Some of the plant stems will be closer to you, while others will be progressively further away. How do we know some are further away? How do we judge space? These become critical problems,

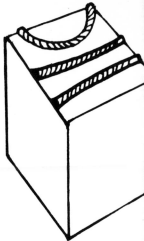

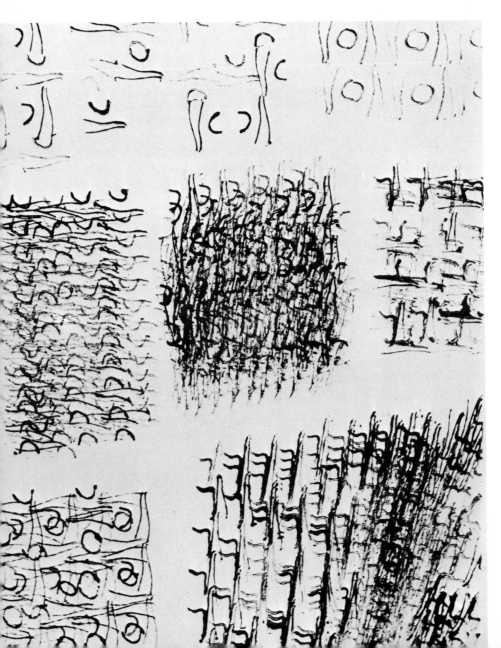

16 Make a simple printing block by gluing a piece of string onto a small block of wood. For maximum versatility don't make the arrangement of string too complex or formal

17 Prints made with string printing blocks

18 Line expressed through embroidery stitches

which confuse many people when they try to interpret spatial effects within a drawing or design.

There are a number of ways of considering space and its interpretation on a flat surface, although some approaches do prove to be interrelated. Objects which are close to us present a much higher level of contrast, between one element and another and between a light and a dark area, and are larger in scale than those which are further away. Plants in a garden illustrate these points. Those close to us can be seen in detail: the light and shade of the stems, the vein structure of the leaves and the manner in which one group of leaves can stand out from other formations. In the middle distance similar plants are less well defined and the level of contrast has diminished. In the far distance outlines are still visible, you are still aware of the overall character of the plant, but it blends much more with others to take its place as part of the landscape.

Photography can illustrate space in a harsh manner to the unwary. The camera lens having no human corrective powers allows objects close to the lens to appear huge, out of all proportion to the rest of the subject. Sometimes fashion photographers have used this effect deliberately to emphasize a feature of an outfit, while amateur photographers produce snapshots of huge feet, large noses or unflattering figures, because they are unaware of it. Spatial qualities exist in even the smallest of objects; shells, plant stems, flowers or rock surfaces. These can be interpreted in a stimulating way through photography, by placing one area in focus, while the foreground and background areas become progressively blurred.

Why bother to learn to draw? It's a question asked by many people. My answer would be that it inspires confidence at a personal level and provides a

19 A 'first' drawing, with a sharp stick and black ink

method of conveying ideas to other people. Perhaps most important of all, it is a useful tool whereby you can learn to analyse design problems. Drawing is very much concerned with looking; it is not so much a matter of deciding how you should draw, but how you should see. It is interesting to look at the drawing made by Erté in 1922 as a design for a bathing costume. He conveys the whole essence of his idea in an almost timeless manner, which rests on a most sympathetic understanding of line shape and proportion and in many ways epitomizes the qualities of perception we have been discussing.

Now you know what you should be looking for, how about making a drawing? Use a soft pencil or pen and ink. Whichever method you choose do not make any preliminary drawing. In the early stages you will no doubt place lines in the wrong positions. Draw over your mistakes, as these lines will help you when positioning later lines. Select a subject with care, choosing one which depends upon line for structure and character, and, most important of all, spend some time studying it before starting to draw. Allow your study to become an analysis of the structure which should be interpreted in line alone. This will force you to be selective. Finally, work boldly, making your drawing as large as possible. Surprisingly enough it is easier this way as there is less inclination on the part of the draughtsman to gloss over important details.

The drawings shown here illustrate what can be done when people work in the manner we have been discussing. The drawings are different in style, but each person has been trying to interpret the plant in front of them through an earnest application of an analytical process uninfluenced by style. Anything is possible; see how you manage.

20 Try to create as many different kinds of line as possi[ble] Experiment with a variety of materials, such as pens, brush[es] sticks and the edge of a ruler

21 Pencil drawing, made on a large sheet of paper

22 Bathing costume designed by Erté in 1922

4 *Shape and Form*

An aspect of design many people might consider even more important than line, is shape and form. Most people like to think they are aware of shape and will quite readily pass judgement on the merits of familiar shapes while they will not even bestow a cursory glance on unusual ones. There are many designs for both embroidery and fashion which are spoiled in their formative stages through ignorance of the role played by these elements, for in many cases shape and form provide structure on which the remainder of the design may be constructed.

A common enough example can be provided by an embroiderer starting a new design. So often the first stage consists of placing a number of ill conceived shapes onto her background fabric. The colour of the fabrics might be quite stimulating and the texture or surface quality of the materials and stitchery employed might work very well. But as soon as the design is well on its way to completion she realizes something is wrong. So many parts of the design are now permanent that alterations to one area would throw other areas out of balance. What has to be done? The usual remedy is either to add more stitchery or step up the level of visual interest by adding beads or glitter to camouflage the original error.

Within the fashion context the problem is even more acute. The ideal shape of a beautiful woman has undergone some surprising changes during the last seventy years. The 'beauty' of the 1900s had an hour-glass shape, a large bust, very small waist and well rounded hips, which were ideally the same measurement as the bust, a sharp contrast with the much lighter, slimmer, 'natural' figure of today. Only since the 1930s have legs been emphasized, reaching the ultimate in display with the mini skirt, when the ideal of long, slender legs demanded an almost impossibly well proportioned shape. While legs became the important erogenous zone, breasts practically disappeared, only to reappear as hemlines descended once more. Breasts have changed their ideal shape from being uniformly moulded in firm, pointed bras to the soft, 'natural' look and then to no support at all, demanded by the see-through look. Again natural perfection was required, not an original idea – look at the Empire Line of the early nineteenth century. With these changes of emphasis the balance of the silhouette will also change. Many people are unaware of this, and see an outfit as a series of isolated shapes, and not as a total image. Again, individual errors, such as wrong shoes or too-short trousers or skirt can completely destroy the balance of a whole outfit.

Unfortunately, many terms we quite happily use in design can be open to many changes in emphasis in their interpretation. Form is one such word. I like to consider it as a three-dimensional development of shape. A simple

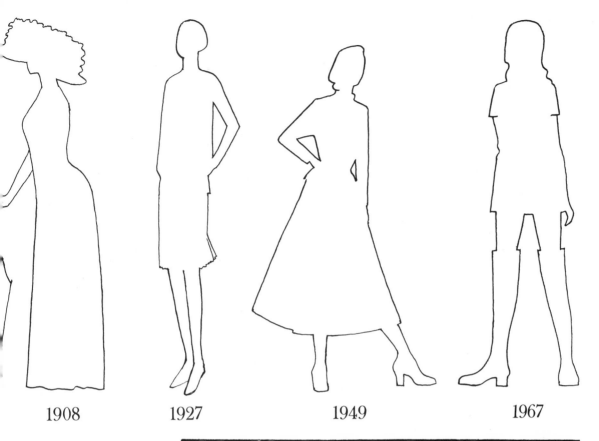

1908 1927 1949 1967

The ideal shape of a beautiful
woman undergoes some surprising
changes

Pantaloon gown with tassels
designed by Poiret, April 1911. A
drawing in which shape is sensitively
identified

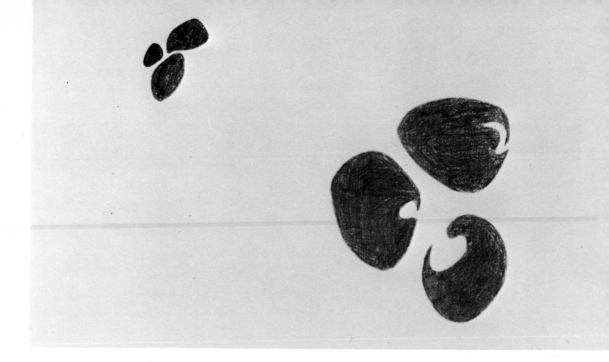

experiment could help to clarify this point. Hold an egg between your fingers so that a light may be used to project the egg's shadow onto a wall. You will notice the shadow has two dimensions, length and breadth, while the egg itself has an extra dimension, which is its depth from front to back. An egg is a symmetrical object; with less regular objects this will not be the case. Having three dimensions we are able to determine the extent of the form in terms of its mass and volume. We can become further aware of two factors which are interrelated but provide differing sensations; first, the space displaced by the egg and second, should the egg be empty, the space enclosed by the egg.

Before we become too involved in what might appear to be rather complex ideas on shape and form, let us return to a more basic position. Most people are aware of shapes and therefore feel they know something of their function. Their thoughts might simply extend to shapes which are familiar and to those which they prefer to the exclusion of all others. Their liking for particular shapes will have been greatly influenced by, first of all, their home background, by the era in which they first began to 'spread their wings' as a teenager and later by furnishing their first home. So very often it is the influence of the first twenty-five years of a person's life which forms the mould for future discrimination. This depends very much upon the extent of influences at that time, on how receptive a person is to shape and form, and changes of concept which are being continually fed into the mix. Even with most enlightened beginnings, people can very easily become either set in their ways or simply resort to tunnel vision, becoming highly motivated only towards certain aspects of shapes and form.

Through experiment I would like you to broaden your concept of this area of design. Whether you consider yourself a person with discrimination or are relatively inexperienced, it is valuable to come to a simple starting position so that your own awareness may begin to extend beyond the limits which you have subconsciously set yourself.

25 and 26 Two experime with freely drawn shapes exploit the balance of a sm mass against a larger one associated with the develo of a family identity

30

Contrasts can once more provide us with useful tools to carry out our research. There are many shapes which might be considered in this way, but two basic categories stand out: the freely formed and the geometrically constructed shape.

I think we all like to experience the sensation of holding a worn pebble in our hands; through touch we explore its water-washed surfaces. We perhaps admire visually the manner in which the surfaces flow, how one particular line of its profile meets, or provides contrast with, another. Yet we need to reassure ourselves by exploring it further with our hands. In this way we begin to feel for the shape of the stone. We become identified with it, as if it were a phrase of music we are particularly fond of. A sculptor can create a similar form out of a block of plaster, or wood, which could be wholly appreciated and understood, if need be, by touch alone. His approach to the problem would be quite straightforward, as far as he is concerned, gradually relating one part of the form to another by cutting, filing and sanding. I do not mean to suggest that the development of the design would move forward without a hitch; it is more than likely many solutions would be tried and rejected, as one modification after another is fed into the process. The sculptor is aware of every change of surface or direction, from flat to convex or concave areas. He is in complete sympathy with each small part of the design and is aware of its impact on the whole form.

Shape may be explored in very much the same way, for instead of subtracting parts of the mass, a shape can be created through a process of addition. Using a soft pencil, make a dot on a sheet of paper. Gradually enlarge this dot with about the same degree of deliberation which you might use when creating a doodle on the back of an old envelope. This does not mean no thought is required, but rather that you need to work in a relaxed manner, in order to allow the dot to grow, through a combination of thinking and doing. Become completely absorbed in the problem instead of working the idea out in your mind before placing on the paper a complete solution. For better or worse the dot will soon develop a personality, or character of its own. Just because it possesses a distinct character does not mean all is well. It might be incoherent, one part having little relationship to another, be so perfectly balanced as to be dull and uninteresting, or be a shape which you always tend to visualize. These are negative qualities. Quite by chance there might be some positive ones as well, which through looking at shape from your usual view-point, you have failed to recognize. Does one particular part of the mass or contour stir the imagination? If so, this is the key to the identity of the shape. Should the essence of this idea be allowed to pervade the whole of the image, you might find to your surprise a shape which you haven't made or seen before. There might be others which are similar, but not the same. If you allow the dot to grow slowly, keeping it as black as possible, many differing versions of the shape can be made as modifications are fed into the system.

Perhaps one danger is that too many ideas emerge and it is therefore not unusual to find people wanting to include them all in a design, to broadcast the brilliance of their inventiveness. How many times have you been aware of this happening when people are considering dress? The designer tries to synthesize an idea through eliminating parts which do not perform any real function. At first sight creating a dot appears to present few problems, but as you perhaps now realize there are many fundamental issues which play an important role in design development. Don't be overawed by these; see them as useful aids which can slowly help your ideas to mature and the shape you are creating to develop form.

Now this is another interpretation of the word form, in this instance signifying the way in which the intrinsic elements of the shape come together to provide a complete, coherent structure. This might manifest itself through the shape looking correct, or in some inexplicable fashion appearing to balance, with or without a symmetrical structural basis.

After having created one shape, which could be fairly large, about 10 cm (4 inches) at its widest point, see what happens when similar shapes are placed near to the first. Build each one up from a dot with the same care and delibera-tion employed for the first shape. Your aim should be to try to preserve the

27 While considering freel drawn shapes, created from memory, it is worth lookin similar shapes formed by a mixture of indian ink and o a glass 35 mm photographic slide

Rose petals can demonstrate interesting qualities of shape and line

A paper collage of an artichoke on a large sheet of paper, illustrates a further method of looking at shape

family likeness, while still trying to make each one different. Spaces between the shapes become crucial, and as with line the background takes a most prominent role in the proceedings. Again positive (shape applied) and negative (the background shapes) are factors which come into play. Very small spaces can give the impression of units pulling together, while on other occasions shapes can be made to appear as if they were moving apart.

Geometric shapes are easier to handle. Firstly their form is more predictable, many being universally recognized. Let us use one of these, the square as the basis of our experiments. Squares can be of different sizes and they can be solid or open, being defined only by line. The solid square may be made to appear lighter than usual, through the surface being broken up with pattern or softened with texture. Colour is another factor, which can be considered later, for again the nature of the square may change through the relationship of the colour of the square to its neighbours.

Using another sheet of paper, a pencil and ruler, create a compact arrangement of squares, without any of them overlapping, to develop a feeling of structure, relating one square to another and so on to the complete whole.

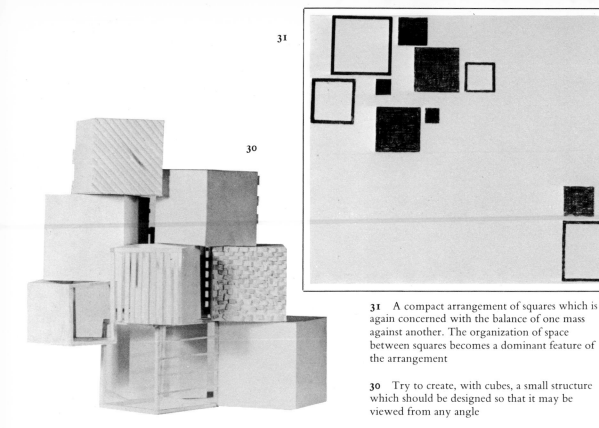

31 A compact arrangement of squares which is again concerned with the balance of one mass against another. The organization of space between squares becomes a dominant feature of the arrangement

30 Try to create, with cubes, a small structure which should be designed so that it may be viewed from any angle

This is not intended to be an obscure, esoteric problem. Again, the issues involved are very simple and yet are fundamental to many problems which occur over and over again.

A stone wall can convey, even to the casual observer, a strong image of structure. The craftsman selects each stone with care. Should the stones have been cut and shaped before use, very elegant arrangements can be achieved, while rougher stones create walls with an equally distinctive character. In each instance while the stones might be of unequal size the line formed by the joints, whether or not they are filled with mortar, is the key to their visual unity. Another stabilizing factor is the predominant horizontal lie of the stones coupled with the less important secondary line of the vertical joints.

If you think of the example of a wall, while you are assembling your structure, you will find the horizontal and vertical stresses of your structure will relate naturally to the vertical and horizontal edges of your paper, giving your design a much needed stability. Stability of structure is an important consideration. Squares need not be absolutely level; they may be tilted and still maintain their stability. How much movement to allow is very much the crux of the problem – as you discovered when we were experimenting with tilted straight lines.

Eventually you could make quite a number of experiments along this theme, making some very formal, others more random, while another approach would be to explore spatial effects, where some squares could appear to recede into, or advance from the paper's surface. Later experiments could use colour or squares made from selected fabrics, papers or card to mobilize the effect of colour on surface quality.

Add a third dimension to a square and it becomes a cube. Instead of considering a nest of square shapes, we can, by means of this added dimension, have a group of cubes which present us with a new problem. Once again scale is vital, for the cubes could be very small, as, for example, part of some exquisite piece of modern jewelry, or they could be very much larger, perhaps forming the basis of an embroidery using geometric forms, a piece of sculpture, or even part of a building.

These examples pose problems similar to those considered through the relationship of squares. But once again it is not the unit, but the space surrounding it, which is important. The balance or interaction between one volume of space and another and the element of surprise which might be engendered through the interaction of these volumes are qualities we are looking for.

These qualities can be experienced in a simple way by initially making two cubes of equal size out of white drawing paper. These may be placed on a white surface and positioned fairly close to one another under a table lamp, which could be used to throw the group into areas of light and shade. Look down onto the group from above so that they appear to be two squares and relate your earlier experience with squares to this new situation. Now slowly change your viewpoint until your eyes are just above the level of the paper. The cubes now appear to be quite large, while the area between the cubes appears to be of even greater significance looking somewhat like the space enclosed by the vertical surfaces of buildings. By changing your eye level you will also change the scale of the cubes. Rotate the group and new vistas will appear, until finally you return once more to your starting point. Change the space between the cubes; angle the position on one cube to another to draw interest to the point where the two cubes interact. From certain angles the eye might not be able to see through the space, but the notion of more space around the corner still exists. This often happens quite by accident in villages which have grown over the centuries. The view along the main village street may be blocked by a tree or bend in the road and this adds considerable interest to the view and increases our speculation about the part of the vista we can't see.

When you have realized what can be achieved with two cubes, see what can be done with more cubes of differing sizes. Try to create, with cubes, a small

32 A further exploration of structure – a drawing of a similar structure, three dimensional forms seen in two dimensions, with pattern and texture.

structure designed so that it may be viewed from any angle, including above and below, enclosing space and containing some of the eye-stopping vistas of the kind we have just discussed.

What a list, but again not as difficult as it sounds! However, it does emphasize the need to look at three dimensional forms from every angle. How many times, for example, has a new dress been visualized from only one viewpoint, usually the front or back?

Your group of cubes may be as large or as small as you wish; don't rush into the gluing stage and try to position your cubes so that you enclose space rather than construct a mass of small cubes round a large one. A useful variation would be to build cubes from fine balsa wood, about the diameter of a matchstick. There are more permutations which are worth considering, relating to the surface of cubes. These include decorating with simple pattern, either in monochrome or colour, or pattern in low relief made from thin card or balsa wood.

Through these experiments you will no doubt become more aware of shape and form, perhaps beginning to feel some relationship between ourselves and architectural space. This is not a new idea, but one which has been around for some time. For example in Japan the Katsura Rikyū, built during the late sixteenth and seventeenth centuries, forms an excellent example of integrated design. The garden relates to the villa, the rooms of which are a sophisticated example of design based on a basic proportional module. They were not considered furnished until occupied and so the form and dress of the occupants was quite consciously absorbed into the integrated space of the structure.

33 The Katsura Rikyū, Japan built during the late sixteenth and seventeenth centuries, forms an excellent example of integrated design

5 *Pattern*

Pattern is an important element of our surroundings. Together with texture it satisfies intensely human needs in what might otherwise be an impersonal, clinical world. For as well as exploring and creating our environment in a visual sense, we need and rely on touch to substantiate our visual findings. To me the world of science fiction is one which concentrates on form, shape and colour without natural surfaces, textures and patterns, a world where sensual experiences have been rationalized out, substituted by standardized solutions and plastic everything.

Reactions to pattern and texture can be strongly influenced by such external factors as climate. In a tropical climate there is little need for soft textures which provide a buffer and insulator against the harsh elements of temperate and cooler zones. In warm areas texture is less important while varieties of pattern help to break up surfaces which might otherwise glare in the strong sunlight, need perforating to allow a breeze to move warm, still air, or provide gentle shade from the sun. The conditioning process can be quite subtle and very few people realize how it affects their preferences for certain kinds of design.

Imagine a continuous graduated scale, with pattern at one end and fine texture at the other. Somewhere along this scale is a hazy region where you might be looking at pattern *or* texture. Scale exerts considerable influence at this point. Walk up to a tree, examine the leaves and note the manner in which they grow on fine stems and how these relate to the branches and so to the trunk. The profile and surface of each species will have its own distinctive appearance, due to the arrangement of leaves, stems and branches, which all form a particular kind of pattern. Now walk away from the tree; the individual pattern of the leaves is no longer visible and the profile of the tree presents a broken surface of light and dark units which cannot be examined separately. Its surface is now a texture, although the exact point at which this has taken place will very much depend upon the eyesight of the viewer. Although we like to identify texture by touch, this is not always possible – it would be very difficult to assess the texture of the leaves by using your hands.

Pattern is used by man to enrich surfaces, to make plain surfaces more interesting, decorative and stimulating, while in the animal world pattern often serves as camouflage, modifying the shape of the insect or animal so that it will blend with its surroundings.

There is a basic human desire for adornment. Primitive people sometimes decorate themselves with pigments or ornaments for ritualistic occasions such as fertility rites or funerals; other civilizations have used pattern on all kinds of objects. The more highly regarded the article, the more it tends to be

The back of a traditional, ghly decorated calabash oon, 27 cm ($10\frac{5}{8}$ inches) high, om West Africa

35 Hundred-*srang* banknote from Tibet, hand printed on r paper

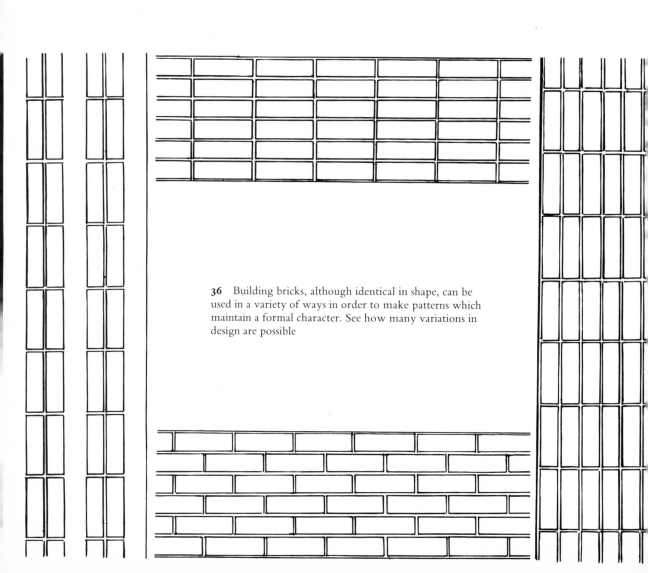

36 Building bricks, although identical in shape, can be used in a variety of ways in order to make patterns which maintain a formal character. See how many variations in design are possible

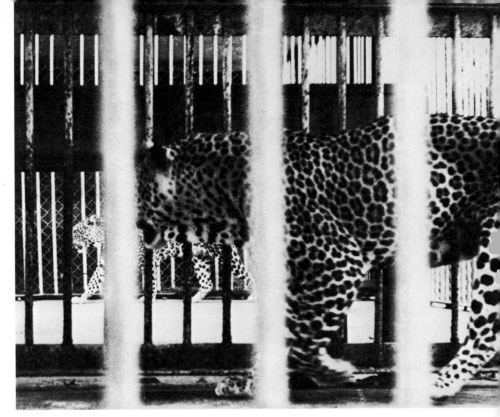

Many forms of pattern can
seen here, extending from
e animals to the structure of
e cage

8 Traditional gold jewelry
orms, 25 mm (1 inch) in
iameter, from Ghana

decorated. The tradition for decoration becomes, over many years, a staple
ingredient of primitive societies at a level which has since been lost by industrialized societies. However, pattern still occupies a key role in our lives, for
the basic primitive needs are still there, although they might be expressed in
different ways.

Pattern as used in fashion and embroidery draws on a wide range of sources.
Many of these are outside textiles and costume and some may be traditional in
the sense of having been used many times in the past. It will be interesting later
to explore some of these sources when thinking of starting points for new
ideas. At the same time you might notice how often the concept of the negative
and positive image, which we have previously discussed, crops up as the key
to pattern.

Most people tend to consider pattern as a design which consists of a single
unit repeated many times in a formal manner. Perhaps the simplest illustration
of this aspect of pattern is building bricks. Each brick is identical in size and
overall colour and the mortar is the same width between each brick. Once you
have seen one part of the pattern it is easy to guess the appearance of the next
section. Bricks, although identical in shape, can be used in a variety of ways to
make patterns which still maintain a formal character. They can, for example,
be stood on end with straight joints or with horizontal joints dropped half
the depth of a brick, or arranged in a herringbone pattern. In these examples
the space between the bricks is constant, but consider the range of options
available as soon as the space between the bricks is no longer constant.

At this point, try some experiments with pattern, starting with simple

39

brick shapes. See how many variations in design are possible. Start by keeping spaces constant, then notice how many more designs are possible when spaces are altered by even minor alterations.

Some formal patterns may contain free, curved shapes. Their formality might be due to strong symmetrical tendencies, as with a roundel window in a cathedral, or an enlarged cross-section of a plant stem, where the cell structure is clearly visible. The predictability of many of these patterns can be altered or destroyed through colour, which could be instrumental in providing greater variety and subtlety of interest. Therefore, even though one might describe a pattern as being formal and perhaps in a particular context un-interesting, in another version it might be very stimulating.

Another category of pattern might be called free pattern. Although many of its characteristics are much the same as formal pattern, it presents a much more spontaneous, expressive appearance. There are many ways in which spontaneity might be achieved. The overall character of the shapes used might be the same as those used for formal patterns, but the intervals between these units might be far from rigid, having been considered in a free, intuitive manner and placed in positions where they immediately look right. The illustrations of small portions of a Ghanaian *adinkra* cloth show this quality. The pattern shapes are printed from carved stamps made from calabash gourds. These are used with thick, black ink to print the design onto cotton.

39 Large and small letter for used in a paper collage study a portion of a sea shell

40 Islamic pattern forms use as the basis of a fabric collage

39 40

41 and 42   Small portions of Ghanaian *adinkra* cloth featuring strong, intuitive pattern

41   42

A small part of a patterned
ic transformed through the
al nature of its folds

All the areas of pattern are swiftly and deftly formed to provide a vibrant, spontaneous pattern which looks absolutely right. Pattern making by children can also possess similar qualities, which can only be partly explained by their direct approach. You, too, could find this method an interesting way of creating pattern, using simple printing blocks made from either wood or lino.

Some examples of experimental weaving have the same spontaneity, the warp and weft structure providing a basis on which the freer elements of the design might be developed. This technique can be used to good effect, especially if it is done on a large scale, which enables ideas to progress quickly. Materials such as string, cord, rope, raffia, cane, wood, metal and plastics offer considerable scope for experiment. These experiments need not attempt to represent any particular form of object, although some might be thought of in terms of screens or hangings. Should they be made sufficiently open in character, like drawn thread work, they could present quite a dramatic appearance when viewed against a strong back light.

Random pattern, another stage in my attempt to classify various forms of pattern, appears to contradict all the tenets of popular theories of pattern. There is no regular break-up of surface and the forms might appear to be very irregular with no distinct reference to repeats. In some instances these characteristics might be considered the prerequisites of texture, but as I mentioned before, scale is an important consideration when we are differentiating between pattern and texture. Long grass blown in a gentle breeze provides a useful example of this kind of pattern; its form is not static, the stems bow before the

44 and **45**   Contrasts in nature: the
very formal design of radiating palm
fronds you see when looking up into a
coconut palm, and a typical random
pattern, as you can see in many trees

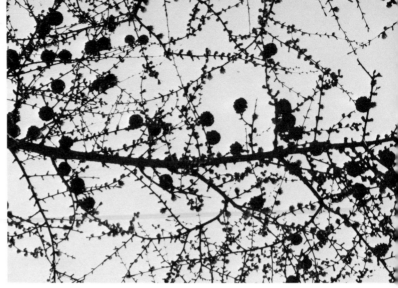

44

wind, and when there is a lull they return to their former position. Another
example, which you no doubt have often noticed, is cloud formations,
especially where low clouds are moving across a pattern of much smaller,
higher clouds. There are many more illustrations which you could find to
describe random pattern which can be identified by its spontaneous or fleeting
nature.

Sometimes these qualities are used in a design, in a dress, for example. The
designer doesn't create the pattern, but creates the opportunity for it to
materialize through the selection and cut of fabric.

Pleats change the character of a design as we have already seen when we were
looking at line, but there are other ways of doing this, such as using semi-
transparent fabric which gives soft folds that move with the wearer, and
produce a spontaneous pattern. Obviously this kind of effect works best when
soft, flowing lines are in vogue, as seen in some of the designs produced by
Bill Gibb and Zandra Rhodes in the early 1970s. Similar designs were evolved
in the 1930s when there was a strong feeling for soft lines and sheer fabrics.

45

6 *Texture*

As we have already seen, the dividing line between pattern and texture is a confused one, although we are certain of one point – it is concerned with surfaces. Perhaps one of the most startling art forms ever made was Meret Oppenheim's cup, saucer and spoon, which were quite ordinary in form and shape but covered entirely with fur. This concept is immediately repulsive to our senses; we feel how uncomfortable it would be to drink from the cup and get a mouthful of fur, where we would normally expect a smooth, clean surface. Our sense of touch is so highly developed that we don't need the physical experience of actually touching the cup to react to the fur. Meret Oppenheim was trading on this reaction; his aim was to outrage and shock the public first by making the cup and saucer an art form and second, by covering them with such a totally unexpected surface. Other surfaces, switched in this manner, would be equally shocking. In the 'right' context fur becomes a most desirable surface, an opulent status symbol, warm and protective. Fur is soft to touch and most desirable to regions of the body other than the tongue. By taking fur as an example of our reaction to surfaces, we see how the same surface may evoke widely contrasting responses.

As infants we begin to explore our surroundings through touch. We continue to add to our vocabulary of forms and textures as we grow up. As with aspects of our visual experience we don't always need to keep adding to our list of textures in order to lead normal, active lives. We see a tree as a tree

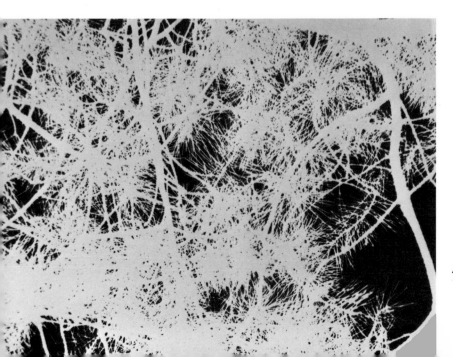

46　Texture seen in a tree

because of its shape and overall texture. Unless we are particularly interested in differentiating between one tree and another, we are not going to notice how the surface texture of one species differs from another. How many people are aware of the different surfaces they walk over during the course of a day? They might on a cold morning in winter avoid slippery ice patches and so take more notice of the ground than usual. In summer walking barefoot over a beach they are likely to become aware of many changes of surface simply because stones can hurt the feet, coarse sand can be unpleasant, while warm dry sand can be a delight.

Unless you regularly enjoy walking barefoot, the experience can be a painful one which can become indelibly printed on your memory. Let us use this as a starting point in our exploration of texture. Once again the best way of doing this is by practical experiment using a variety of different materials of which some of the simplest are poster or polymer acrylic colours. Often when asked to recreate an experience from memory we so telescope our reactions that they are recalled in a highly concentrated form. With memories of walking barefoot try to recreate a rough, coarse texture using paint on either a black or white sheet of paper. Try to project your idea in the way an actor tries to project an idea to an audience, by presenting it larger than life size. This does not mean you should enlarge the texture but rather concentrate on the emotional response to it. Forget all about colour and develop the idea in monochrome. In this way the main problem of reproducing light and shade to describe the feeling of surface begins to come through. There are two ways in which the surface may be reproduced. One is by mixing coarse materials with paint in order almost to model the surface. The second method, which is much more rewarding in the long run, is partially to develop the topographical surface of peaks and hollows, allow the paint to dry and then shade or draw into it using a black or white crayon or a soft pencil. While you are doing this, concentrate on your reaction to this kind of surface, working to and fro across its area, intently and rapidly intensifying the surface until you think you have reproduced the feelings which exist in your mind. You may be surprised to find that this might take some time to achieve.

After you have attempted to create this surface, return again to thoughts of the beach, but this time try to manufacture the opposite of the previous texture. Choose a texture which is triggered off by pleasant memories of warm, soft, smooth sand. To mix sand with white or black paint would not reproduce this surface but give you a hard, abrasive texture. The idea you need to explore is an abstract one. Your reaction to the sand is not photographic, but an expression of muddled, perhaps prejudiced feelings. This is very much our reaction to all surfaces.

More experiment will certainly heighten your reaction and receptiveness to texture. You will notice texture in the garden, on your way to work, when shopping or in the house. Some textures you might have seen daily and simply used them for purposes of recognition, but now they begin to take on a new significance.

Test your reactions by making a collection of ten to fifteen rubbings of surfaces in your vicinity. Most people have made rubbings at one time or another when they were children; the process is not difficult, but it does require some care if you are to obtain sharp black and white results. You need sheets of thin, white paper and a few sticks of thick, black crayons made

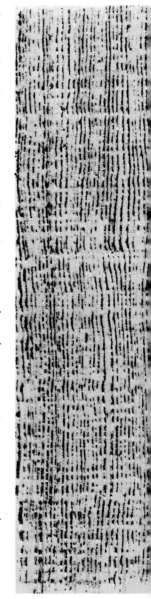

xtend your awareness of texture by making a series
bings of surfaces within your vicinity. Here are two
on surfaces, wood (left) and concrete (below)

heavily textured stone from the seashore

he rich, textured surface of a rusty boiler

48

49

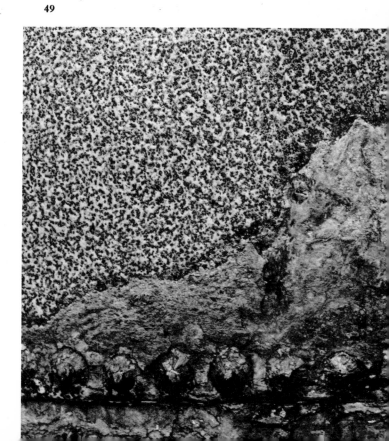

50

51

52

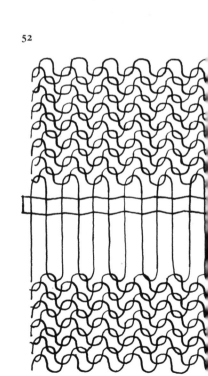

46

specially for this purpose. When you have found a surface which you think might be suitable, clean off any dust or dirt, hold the paper over the most interesting area and then rub over the surface of the paper with the crayon. If you rub evenly and hold the paper firm, the texture beneath will begin to show through. Continue to rub the crayon over the surface until the impression is clear and black. Lay the completed rubbings out on a table. There will be rough ones, smooth ones and some which you could call pattern. In making the rubbings the transparency of glass, coolness of iron and warmth of wood are factors which will have been eliminated. We see the textures only as gradations between black and white. Place your rubbings in family groupings of like qualities. Compare your findings with the original subjects and you will be surprised to see some quite unusual bedfellows and perhaps notice how many of them, even though they came from a wide range of surfaces, are very similar.

By now you might have a very positive reaction to texture, noticing many subtle variations which may be found in a comparatively small area. Many textures are indigenous to particular materials, while others have been designed into the material for aesthetic effect. You can also experiment with texture with the aim of creating a particular kind of appeal, although your goals should be modest at first. Make a small area of fabric with an overall feeling of roughness; later you may progress to experiments aiming for a specific

Plastic bags cut into long
ps provide another knitting
erial. It is surprising to feel
transformation of the surface
e the material has been
ted

Texture created by string
ting could provide ideas for
hine embroidery

Creating surfaces through
ting. This diagram illustrates
knitting and weaving
ht be combined

Texture explored through
roidery

53

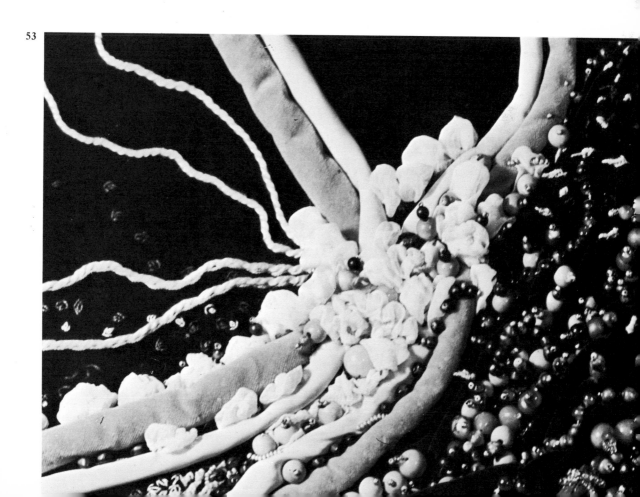

54   55

type of roughness. By using the word fabric I have perhaps already created difficulties; it sounds such a difficult task. This is not so, for when a person takes some wool and knitting needles and starts to knit, she is creating a fabric. So let us start with this idea in mind and make a number of small experimental samples no larger than about 23 cm (9 inches) square. Many of you might find this difficult, not because you can't knit, but because you are so used to using the process in a conventional manner. So, to allow fresh ideas to emerge, use unusual materials and extra-large needles and don't worry if you drop stitches, or make loops in unexpected places, for accidents of this kind may make the surface much more interesting. Thin strips of paper, polythene, string, card, wood-wool packing material, wood shavings and strips of fabric all provide the challenge of something different. When you have done a number of experiments with these unlikely materials, switch your attention to wool and yarns, but incorporate some of the earlier samples.

With this sequence of experiments you have an opportunity to develop your own theme. If your samples have a 'loopy' quality it doesn't matter. There is tremendous scope for experiment here. Changes can be made through altering the scale, inserting rolls of paper to make extra large stitches, changing the size of your needles and deliberately allowing the fabric to develop large holes as part of its character. There is no need to concern yourself with problems of how the fabric may eventually be used, or whether it should have motifs designed into it. The knitting process will provide all the structure you

54 and 55   Contrasting machine embroidery and beadwork

56   Flower painting by a pe who always maintained she couldn't draw

need and the horizontal emphasis of knitting will provide sufficient interest in itself, especially when you recall your earlier experiments with straight lines.

Weaving is the more usual process of making fabrics, although in recent years the knitting process has eroded the supreme position of woven textiles as the prime provider of fabrics. Again weaving can be thought of in either a traditional or experimental manner. I think it is important with all these processes to remember that traditional methods grew out of necessity and experience and need not be the only way to work. All you need to know is the basic principle of the loom, that the horizontal yarns, the weft, move over and under the vertical yarns, the warp. The materials used will influence the character of the fabric: hard materials will make a fabric hard to the touch, while soft materials, such as wool, will make a fabric soft to the touch. Again, to start with the same unfamiliar materials, such as those suggested for knitting, will bring the best results and provide new ideas to set the pace for the time when you go back to more traditional materials. It is very interesting to compare the appearance of samples developed through knitting and those created by weaving. Even though the materials might be the same, the results in terms of handling will probably be totally different.

Texture may be explored in yet another way, embroidery, which after the previous examples might appear more conventional. Here again you should aim to produce something quite unlike anything you may have produced previously and very strongly based on the experiments we have discussed so far. Make a number of small samples about 10 cm (4 inches) square. It is easy to drop into the habit of compartmentalizing experiences, so do use what you have discovered so far, through knitting and weaving, as a basis for your experiments in embroidery. A good way to start would be to use a large needle and string, or some other less conventional material. Each surface could be made through repeating one or two embroidery stitches, feeling the quality of the merging surface in much the same way as experimenting with paint. It would be easy to suggest making surfaces with a great number of different stitches, but I think more is to be gained through deliberately limiting the variety of stitches used and achieving variety of effect through experiment with the scale of stitch, mixing large with small. Machine embroidery is quicker; repetition is a new factor and so naturally extends the scope of this phase of experiment by using stitches and threads which are within the scope of the machine. Free, sensuous surfaces can still be created, but they will be quite different to those made entirely by hand.

I am sure you notice the difference in my approach to the more conventional outlook towards texture in embroidery. Many embroiderers think in terms of the stitches and techniques to be used, referring to a work as having been created through a particular stitch. I think it is much better to think of the nature of the surface first and later, through experiment, find stitches to interpret it.

7 *Colour*

Most adults hold very strong views on how colour should be used and which colours they particularly like or dislike. Young people are less rigid in their choice of colour. They experiment, are influenced by home background and the media, but gradually as they grow older tastes become more rigid and they find themselves drawn towards certain colours which have become comfortable to use, while other more troublesome ones are rejected. So rather than achieving an expansive, mature understanding of colour, they establish a rather more limited pattern, epitomized by, 'I know what I like.'

The fashion industry uses planned obsolescence as a deliberate method of increasing sales. Colour plays a vital role here. We are introduced to 'new' colours which are intended to excite and dramatize and make last season's colours appear old-fashioned and dull. In turn the new colours themselves become overworked, like a popular hit tune, to be discarded in favour of next season's titillating theme. Some people are quite happy to be ruled by the dictates of fashion, to the exclusion of personal preferences and real suitability. With the upsurge of the youth cult in the early 1960s, due in part to increased affluence amongst young people and the ensuing attention of the pop music industry, a unique counter-influence emerged to challenge the status quo of fashion. The sub-culture which blossomed brought many new ideas, one of which was an encouragement for participants to be individuals, 'doing their own thing'. Inevitably this less slavish outlook has become a part of Establishment thinking, throwing greater responsibility on the individual to select and use colour in a way which would best express personality and yet be in step with contemporary social ideas.

Clothing more than embroidery reflects trends in fashionable colour, for although embroidery is itself influenced by social change, its transition is more gradual. Together with other areas of design, it has been influenced by the work of painters, whose ideas crystallize over a period of time and are in no way subjected to a frantic programme of change dictated by commercial interests. The painters who have provided the most significant colour influence on twentieth-century design are the Impressionists. Impressionism drew attention to a new way of looking at the environment; it emphasized the role played by colour and light, releasing colour from an academic tradition of being always subservient to form, to become a dominating feature in its own right. Colour experiment has since spread into other areas of design, so that today architecture, interior decoration, advertising, clothing, cars and even engineering tools all display exciting, vibrant colour. There is perhaps so much colour about that we now fail to notice much of it, returning once more to the maxim of seeing only what we want to see.

7 Jagged, horizontal bands of olour used to explore colour lationships

It was during the seventeenth century that Isaac Newton first demonstrated that white light was the source of colour. He shone a beam of white light through a glass prism, which refracted or bent the ray so that it broke down into its constituent parts, which proved to be the colours of the rainbow: red, orange, yellow, green, blue and violet. What made his experiment even more conclusive was his ability to re-form the ray of white light by passing the coloured rays through a second prism. Light rays are responsible for all the colours we see. For example, a car is red because its pigment absorbs all the colours of the spectrum apart from red, which it reflects. A white surface is white because it reflects all the colours, so that, as Isaac Newton demonstrated, we see white light.

Newton's colours form what we now call the prismatic colour circle, which in its simplest form consists of six colours. These are divided into two groups: primary (red, yellow and blue) and secondary (orange, green and violet). The primary are basic colours, not formed from a mixture of other colours, while secondary colours are formed from an equal mixture of two primary colours. By adding a third group, tertiary colours, formed by mixing a primary with a secondary colour, the circle grows to comprise twelve colours. Colours which are opposite to one another in the colour circle are

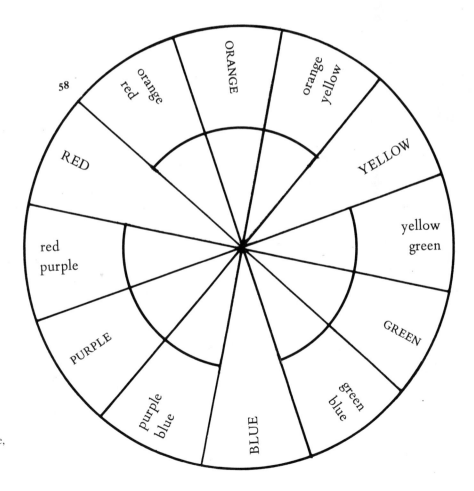

The prismatic colour circle, owing primary, secondary d tertiary colours

known as complementary colours; for example, the complementary of red is green. When all the primaries are mixed together you get a neutral grey and not white as you might expect.

This brings us to another way in which colours might be mixed – optically, within the mechanism of the eye. Consider blobs of pure primary colours placed next to each other, in varying proportions, against a white background. Blobs of yellow interspersed with blobs of blue appear as green when viewed at sufficient distance to enable the individual blobs to merge. Colour used in this way gives brighter, purer hues. Pigments, no matter how well manufactured, are impure; that is why when complementaries are mixed together we get a grey instead of white. Pointillist painters Seurat and Signac, nineteenth-century followers of the Impressionist tradition, used this theory to enhance the brightness and purity of their colour. You don't have to look far to find contemporary applications of this principle. The most familiar of these, the reproduction of colour photographs in books and magazines, relies upon the photographic breakdown of coloured images into dots. The colours, yellow, red and blue are used as well as black, which provides greys. Greys add substance to colours and also break down any harshness that might arise from using only three colours. As colour television works on a similar principle, minus the black, you have no doubt become aware of the over-bright colours which demonstrate the weaknesses of the three-colour system. These three colours are in fact a little different from the three primaries. In this system yellow is replaced by green, so the three colours are red, green and blue; they are known as the additive primary colours. For when these overlap, we get the white light which Isaac Newton obtained with his prism. I would suggest it is sufficient just to know of the existence of this system, which today is hardly remote from everyday experience; it is of little immediate value when considering colour in design.

There is no doubt that one of the ways of understanding colour is through experiment. It can be a help to use available colour sometimes but it does not provide the rich experience which can be obtained through colour mixing. A good starting point would be to make yourself a prismatic colour circle, 15 cm (6 inches) in diameter. While you are making the colour circle, paint an extra area of each colour onto a spare piece of white paper. These can be made into colour samples for use in later experiments.

From the very beginning try to lay down colour well. Mix the pigments thoroughly, so that they are neither too watery and transparent, nor too thick. Flat areas of colour with clean, sharp edges are required. This is not difficult to manage if you use a good quality, medium sized, sable brush and easily applied colour such as poster colour or designer's gouache (a more refined version of poster colour). Watercolour would be too difficult to use at this point, but later, when you want transparent effects, it will most certainly come into its own. Don't allow any hard pencil lines to come between areas of colour; to see how one colour can influence another you must put the colours next to one another.

The American colourist Albert Munsell, during the early years of the twentieth century, was engaged in research into a system of colour notation which he hoped could match the system of notation used in music. His solution is an interesting one, which does serve to pinpoint the three-dimensional nature of colour. He distinguished three dimensions which he called hue, tone,

59 The additive primary system: red, green and blue. Where these three colours overlap we have white light

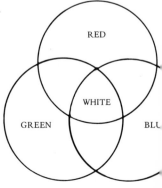

and chroma. Hue, the quality by which we distinguish one colour from another, is straightforward and quite easily understood. The second dimension, tone, the quality of brightness, is easier to see in some colours than in others. For example, yellow is brighter than violet, but is red brighter than green? The third dimension is chroma, the quality of saturation, or measure of colour content. A simple experiment can help you to understand this particular aspect of colour. Place a small amount of water in a saucer, add one brush of pigment, mix thoroughly with the water, and paint the result of this mixture onto a sheet of white paper. Repeat the process many times until the painted panels show no further degree of saturation. The deeper the tone of the colour the longer this scale can become; yellow, being very close to white, will have a relatively short scale, while deeper-toned colour, being closer to black, will provide a much longer scale due to greater tonal contrast.

It is surprising how few people see colour in terms of tone. A number of simple tests on your friends will soon prove this. All you need is a tonal scale running from white to black in ten stages and the set of colour samples you made when painting the colour circle. Now ask your friends to look at the colours in terms of tone alone and to place these against their exact counterparts on the graduated tonal scale. A simple test, but one which will provide many unusual solutions. Another experiment which could be tried at the same time, would be to see if these same colour samples could be arranged in an order from warm to cool. I find that people tend to start from premeditated positions, placing red at one end of the scale and blue at the other. When questioned the stock reply is that red is hot and blue is cold. The remaining colours perhaps get fairer treatment, but are still imprisoned by the choice of the first two colours. Is red always hot? Is blue always cold? There can be blue reds and orange reds, while there can also be very cool, green blues and very hot blues.

The dimensions of colour,
 e, tone and chroma

Extend a colour by adding
 hite, black and water

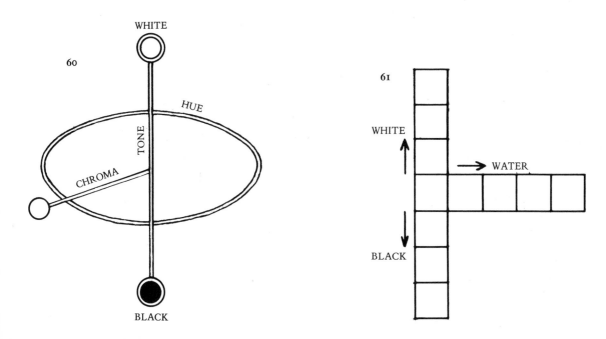

Straight lines offer an opportunity to explore some further characteristics of colour. With line we became aware of the relationship between line and background, the interval between one line and another and how this might be applied to the whole theme of design. Colour can be explored in a similar way, for colour proportion and colour relationships have been rewarding themes in twentieth century design. Painters such as Mondrian, Joseph Albers and Mark Rothko used these qualities as central themes in their work.

Now select a number of different materials with a variety of surface qualities, such as rough, smooth, shiny, dull, transparent or opaque. Narrow your choice to a limited colour range, based on a segment of the colour circle and its complementary colours. You should have no difficulty in finding sufficient materials; they can include paper of varying finishes, plastics and fabric, or anything else as long as it is composed of one colour. In addition, paint a number of broad bands of colour on paper, to provide missing links within your chain of samples if necessary.

Leaving aside the complementary colours for the moment, arrange strips of your samples to form parallel bands of colour. The natural tendency will be to use too many different kinds of material and too broad a range of colour. Gradually narrow your choice until one surface appears to influence, or is affected by, another. You might have the same colour appearing as shiny and rough surfaces; notice how the surface quality affects the appearance of these two so that they look different. Play on this fact, making it an essential feature of the design. As with the earlier arrangement of straight lines, try to create a centre of interest, perhaps by allowing a large area of one colour to be placed in close proximity to a much narrower band of another. These arrangements can be placed on different backgrounds and again surface quality can play a big part. I am sure you will be surprised to notice the degree of change between a shiny card background and a much softer one of the same colour, formed by matt paper or plain fabric. Decide how large the background should become in relation to the horizontal bands of colour, perhaps adjusting the arrangement to allow the background colour to appear as occasional bands of colour. So far you have a design composed entirely of colours originating from one segment of the colour circle. It might have, for example, a predominantly yellow, yellow-green, or green-blue flavour. As the colours have a common denominator and lie close to one another in the colour circle, they relate easily. The problem now is to create enough interest in the arrangement to stop it becoming dull. Adjusting the proportion and surface qualities of the colours will have gone a long way towards avoiding this, and in some instances these qualities alone can provide sufficient variety of interest.

Complementary colours can play a role here. For example, were you to walk into a room where every surface, including the furnishings, was yellow, you might at first be surprised. But gradually this might wear off as your sensitivity towards yellow diminished, while your sensitivity to its complementary, violet, increased. In this case a touch of violet in the colour scheme would immediately bring out the yellowness of yellow, thus providing that spark of interest which would bring the scheme to life. Try the same principle with your own design, but use your complementary colour sparingly and with great care.

Experiment in this way as much as possible, for the more you do, the more sensitive you are likely to become to the opportunities available for imaginative use of colour in fashion and embroidery. The last thirty years have seen great changes in colour usage; no longer are you likely to be discouraged from using certain colours because 'they don't go together,' but on the contrary you are likely to be encouraged to try new colour groupings.

Now let us consider another dimension. How light, or dark, can a colour become and yet retain its characteristic hue? A red mixed with white will gradually become pink and eventually progress to white. Conversely, red mixed with black will gradually become brown, dark brown and finally black. I find many people have difficulty in visualizing, mixing and using light colours (tints) and dark colours (shades), preferring to stay close to clearer hues.

There are many ways in which tints and shades of a colour might be explored. The most common method is to take a colour and extend it by mixing it with one part of white, or black, followed by two parts and then three parts, and so on until a scale of values has been obtained. Another method would be to select and arrange fabrics and other materials in order of lightness or darkness. Both these approaches have limitations; the first is mechanical and limited to a single colour, and the second is restricted through the availability of the materials and overlooks the tremendous amount of information which can be gained through mixing your own colours and dyes.

Colour can possess many moods; it can be light, soft, mysterious, spatial. Images can be made to loom out of a mist of colour, fading away only to be replaced by other images. Focal points expressed through subtle changes of colour and tone can whisper out from the drifting images, lending those slight inflections which arrest a tendency towards a monochromatic dullness.

With this idea in mind, create a design on a large sheet of paper, using extremely soft, gentle colours, in which tone values will be very close to one another. Try to avoid an overall flatness by introducing a focal point, either by making colours lighter than ever, or through careful use of complementary colour. As its main feature will be colour its actual structure can be very simple. You might do this by using horizontal bands of different widths, or by being a little more ambitious, using bands of colour created with a template cut from thick paper. The profile of the template could be jagged, undulated or curved, the interest being created through careful consideration of the variation of interval between lines, as shown in **62**. Your design will gain in strength if the bands of colour stretch from one side of the paper to the other on either a horizontal or vertical axis.

The difficulty you are most likely to encounter is in making your colours light enough – an obvious point, but one well worth considering. Test the colours, allowing them to dry before you apply them to the design. In order to avoid mixing huge quantities of each colour, add pigment to white, or if using dye or watercolour, add pigment to water. Work towards an atmosphere which is as light and dream-like as morning mist. Your earliest attempt is bound to be too dark in tone, so try one or two lighter versions of this idea. Later try the same theme again but this time taking the other end of the scale by using colours that are as dark as possible without being black. Both these experiments should extend your colour range considerably through colour mixing and the extra attention which must be paid to tone values. On their own these studies don't provide a complete means of extending colour awareness, for to a certain extent they are capitalizing on previous experience and prejudices.

Using a template with ɡged lines compose a simple ꜱign

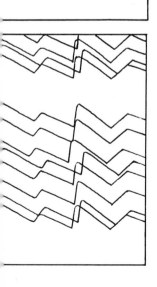

Experience needs to be extended in other directions, first by recognizing how we can all limit ourselves unwittingly through the assumption that everyone sees, or feels for colour in the same way. Let me provide a simple example; imagine walking along a street and becoming engulfed quite suddenly in a noisy crowd of people wearing reddish-brown robes. Imagine becoming involved on another occasion with a group formed up in silent procession, this time wearing black. Perhaps you can guess the link between the two events; both are funerals, the first being part of a traditional ceremony in West Africa and the second in any Christian country. By considering such examples it is possible to see how differences in colour association might arise through religious and social customs.

Environment might also play a part; for example, people who live in areas where there is a lot of green or white have been known to have many more terms to differentiate between various forms of greenness or whiteness. Availability of pigments and dyes can mean that societies have many terms for available colours, but few, or none at all, for colours which we might consider common but which are beyond their experience.

Finally, climate can also effect the way colour is used; bright sunlight drains away its strength, so in hot climates you tend to compensate for this by wearing stronger colours than those normally used in more temperate zones. Sunlight affects surfaces in other ways too. I can recall sitting in a white-walled room with large windows, overlooking a green garden; on bright, sunny days this caused the walls and ceiling to become suffused with a strong green colour. I suppose I was also engulfed by this strong, reflected light which must have changed the colour of my clothing, arms and face. You will no doubt have noticed this effect as well, for reflected light from articles of clothing can change the colour of neck, face and arms.

Perhaps you can understand how colour can prove to be the most interesting, fluid and rewarding aspect of design. I have tried to do nothing more than open a few doors to some of its basic dimensions. A little more time spent in this area by most people would most certainly lead them to produce more scintillating garments and embroideries.

8 *Design through Materials*

The fundamental form of a garment, its accessories and decoration bring together elements which give reality to the concept of design enveloping the human figure. This can be more readily experienced if you experiment with unfamiliar materials in this traditional area, which forms a bridge between elements of design and the development of ideas.

I find many people can quite readily appreciate design when it is broken down into a number of elements, and each is examined in turn. Even when these elements are grouped together in twos and threes their relationships can still be understood. But, as we all tend to place our discoveries in separate compartments, to bring these elements together and mobilize their combined resources in the quest of creating new visual ideas often proves difficult. 'How do I create a new design? I can't think of anything new.' These are the usual cries as someone desperately awaits the assistance of divine power to complete an idea.

People find it easier to think creatively while handling materials which do

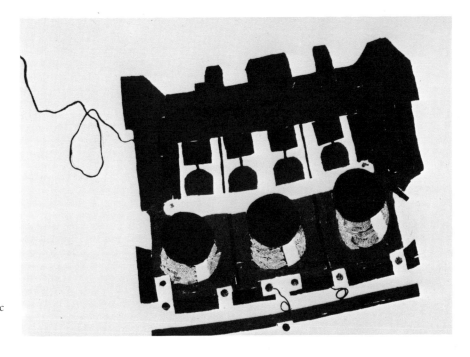

63 Strong shapes in a fabric collage based on electrical components

64 A 'finished dress', developed without patterns – essentially a 'cut and stick' process, using Vilene (interfacing), gold metallic paper and tissue paper

not involve the apparent permanency of drawing and painting. Units can be moved from one place to another before being finally fixed in position. When starting to use materials in this way people have a strong tendency to do it the hard way, making firm decisions too early and fixing units in places that they later regret. The range of materials which might be used is enormous, far too wide to even attempt to catalogue here. But in order to provide a path through this field of abundance there are some ideas which might help to polarize your thoughts.

The most immediate process, when considering design through materials, is collage. Here it is appropriate that it should be made with fabric, although collage can be made from any kind of material, such as fabric, wood, metal, plastic, paper and card, or any combination of these.

An assemblage of more bulky units could be used in a manner similar to low relief, or as a free standing sculptural unit. Components for structures of this kind are not difficult to find, they might be made from basic natural and man made materials, such as seeds, wood, foodstuffs, nails, screws, tacks,

65 You can create a 'finishe dress' using Vilene (interfacir Many helpful ideas are throv up by this experimental 'cut stick' process

60

washers, plastic tubing or other small, plastic oddments. While more bulky parts could originate from metal or plastic containers, or mechanical and electrical components.

Knitting and weaving processes also explore design in this way. These techniques provide different structures which afford many interesting ways of handling materials, for whereas collage and assemblage unite their elements through glueing, welding, or hammering, knitting and weaving can absorb materials into their structure.

All these processes share one point in common, which is fundamental to design as a whole. As the design concept emerges they will shed their original identity gradually to accept a new role dictated by the design. In some areas of design this happens quite easily; for example, wool yarn knits into a sweater, changing through the knitting process into a new form. But with such basic materials as nails, paper clips and metal washers, which are very familiar in their original form, it is quite a challenge to present them in a new image. This is not impossible as long as you remember to recognize these shapes for what they really are: a wire nail is a cylindrical unit capped by a circular disc and a washer is a circular disc with a large round hole. When these are arranged in different ways, pattern and texture of different kinds will result. Nails might be hammered into a block of wood so that the nail heads, apart from being spaced in either a pattern or texture formation, can extend to different heights above the surface of the wood.

Other materials might change their appearance through much more drastic measures. Clear plastic tubing is always a stimulating material to work with. Unfortunately, people don't spend long enough considering its potential. It can be sliced across its diameter to provide rings, ranging from narrow rings like a washer to cylindrical units of any length. The tube might be sliced in half. If so, the pieces can be re-assembled to make an undulating surface which can vary in appearance, depending upon whether the inner or outer surface is upppermost. The pieces can be placed side by side in units of equal length, or cut up into much smaller pieces and arranged without any semblance of order to give a textured surface. Plastic tubing might also be filled with pigment to produce either a fluid or solid coloured core, depending upon the consistency and type of pigment used.

By discussing the possibilities of plastic tubing in this way I have tried to show how one element might be used in many different ways. Through this process you discover a great deal about the nature and potential of the material. So many people working with materials fail to explore the potential of their subject matter, never going beyond their previous knowledge – a nail is a nail, a piece of plastic tubing is plastic tubing. Perhaps it is because they don't try to sort out their ideas in a simple enough manner, trying to express them-selves too figuratively. A paper collage based on a careful study of flower forms might not prove too difficult, for the process and the material would force the designer to look very closely at the flowers in order to evaluate colour, shape, form, pattern and texture, before deciding how best to translate them into a successful collage. The same might be done with other materials, forcing the designer to select more carefully those elements which are intensely characteristic of the subject while also being compatible with the materials being used.

Before embarking upon figurative subject matter, I think it is helpful to

66 Paper collage portrait, which emphasizes the character of the sitter. An opportunity to explore shape, pattern and colour

67 Kippers, another bold paper collage interpretation

Fluid, decorative forms
in dress embroidery

work in purely abstract terms on a small scale. A useful size for experiment is 23 cm (9 inches) square. Think only in terms of areas of tension or interest and how these might relate to the dimension of the square. In other words employ the experience gained so far to develop a design by intuitively selecting and manipulating materials until a successful design emerges. I might have given the impression that you develop the idea through a single type of group of materials; at first a discipline of this nature might not be a bad idea, though later you should begin to experiment with combinations of different materials, sometimes drastically changing their character by clever juxtaposition or by altering their appearance by spraying with paint or dyes.

How can this kind of experience possibly be relevant to a person working within the disciplines of fashion and embroidery? Embroiderers no doubt realize their subject is intensely concerned with surfaces and recognize the value of this work in that it encourages experiment and a rather more positive first stage in idea development. Fashion might seem to gain less from it but in fact the reverse is probably true. Design with materials will certainly increase awareness of the feel and handling of fabrics to a much greater extent than simply working on a flat, painted surface. For softness, opacity, transparency, roughness, crispness, shinyness can all be experienced in an intense manner which will eventually contribute to a more considered selection of fabrics and their place in an overall 'look'. There are times when clothes rely upon applied decoration in the form of dress embroidery or when the total outfit is enhanced by decoration applied to the person in the form of jewelry and these too will benefit from this work.

Jewelry need not always be made of precious stones, pearls, silver or gold,

Symmetrical design com-
d of nails and tacks, 23 cm
ches) square

An assemblage, composed
ils, rings and plastic tubing,
n (9 inches) square

69   70

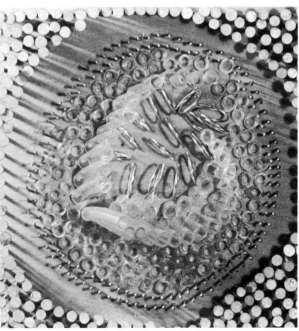

71 and **72** Experimental jewelry
relating design with materials to the
human figure

71   **72**

and it is always more important to consider the decorative effect of jewelry in
terms of the complete fashion image. Instead of limiting design with materials
to a square, start to think of the much more exciting proposition of relating
this kind of design to the human body, as decoration, or, in its more familiar
form, jewelry.

Again, the key to the scheme is to think along original lines, capitalizing on
the experience acquired while working on the small, square panel. Now the

66

background has changed; it is no longer static – new shapes, contours of the neck, head, arms, hands, legs, ankles and feet, now provide a three-dimensional challenge.

No doubt after your first experiments, you can begin to think of many more materials which could be used. Consider adding leather, electric wire with its many colours of insulation material, fuse wire and fine wire of various grades to your list. Always collect many more materials than you are likely to need.

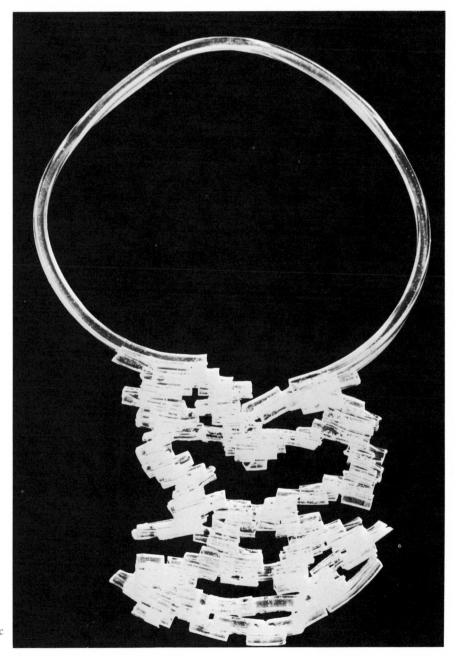

63 Necklace made from plastic tubing

Although it doesn't appear to be too difficult to make original ideas out of these materials, you may very well find that it is. Many people make the mistake of following current fashion trends too closely; much better, less superficial ideas emerge through working more directly through the character of the materials available.

Experiment initially on a flat surface, such as that provided by coloured cards and papers with shiny or matt surfaces. There is a good reason for this, one which you discovered when we were discussing colour, which is the marked difference occurring to the appearance of objects when grouped together in different ways or on a variety of surfaces. Once more it is a probing experience; qualities not immediately discernable gradually emerge, forming embryo ideas which will eventually become the basis of original designs. Once again, if everything is working according to plan, units will begin to gell into a new form, losing their earlier, separate identities.

As soon as you have a number of ideas, which could all be following the same theme, consider how they might be related to the human figure. Only at this stage should you consider how various elements of a design might be linked together so they will indeed fasten around an arm, or hang from a neck. It is quite unnecessary to worry about this problem any earlier and often it restricts original thinking.

This brings us back to the problem of which comes first, concept or technique. This question, posed earlier, will be answered many times in practice; even so I find that when people are aware of this point it continues to go against all previous training to develop an idea without first knowing how it can be made to work. The extra challenge of relating design to the human figure is one of scale; a very heavy design can easily swamp a small, delicate wearer. Other factors relating to scale need very careful attention, especially when you are combining different parts of a design, as in the case of a chain or pendant.

While not totally abandoning decoration through jewelry, let us begin to consider the total look of the figure in terms of design with materials, in which jewelry will play its part. Earlier we discussed simple forms such as cylinders and cones and how these relate to dress shapes. A figure in a long, slinky, tubular floor-length dress is easy to imagine, while the combination of cylindrical and cone shapes is much more subtle. When we·are discussing these terms the softness, cut and weight of the fabric are mellowing factors which can make an extremely simple, basic idea difficult to see.

A tubular form is an ever-recurring theme in dress design. A number of experiments with cylindrical forms will provide a good starting point for our enquiry. I would like you to make a series of cylinders out of white paper; they should be about 23 cm (9 inches) in length by about 10 cm (4 inches) in diameter. Here we have the most basic cylindrical shape. How can it be altered? As far as cutting is concerned, the top and bottom provide areas of immediate interest. When cutting these areas avoid the temptation simply to cut a jagged edge; instead, think very carefully about shape and work directly on the cylinder with a sharp pair of scissors to cut out areas giving form to clean, sculptural shapes. Try to relate the shape carved out of the top of the cylinder to the one created at the bottom, so that they are not necessarily the same but are of compatible form. A number of different ideas can be developed through working along this theme; don't move away from it until you are satisfied all its aspects have been fully explored. The top portion of the cylinder could remain the same while the bottom receives some modification. This could be through developing a single slit, two slits or more. The length of the slits is adjustable, depending upon the effect required, while the base can be considered in two ways, as either rounded or angled. Draw upon your earlier experience of shape. In keeping with previous discussion on developing design through contrasts, make the top and bottom of the cylinder decorative while the middle remains plain. Continuing this theme, keep the outer extremities of the cylinder plain while decorating the central area by cutting holes in the cylinder walls.

Decoration through pattern and colour can also be explored on its own, as a means of breaking up the surface of the cylinder, or together with areas already decorated by cutting. Some cylinders could remain relatively plain with a sculptured look, while others could be much more highly decorated, perhaps exploring colour.

So far you have created a series of cylinders, all initially alike but now quite different. Some might appear more interesting than others. The best will present complete ideas, workable from every angle. Imagine the more successful designs as candidates for enlargement up to human proportions.

Rather than moving too quickly from small to large cylinders it is better to move slowly, working out further ideas on paper. The drawings on the next page illustrate one way of starting this process. Notice how there is little need

Create a series of experi-
tal sculptural forms based
ylinders

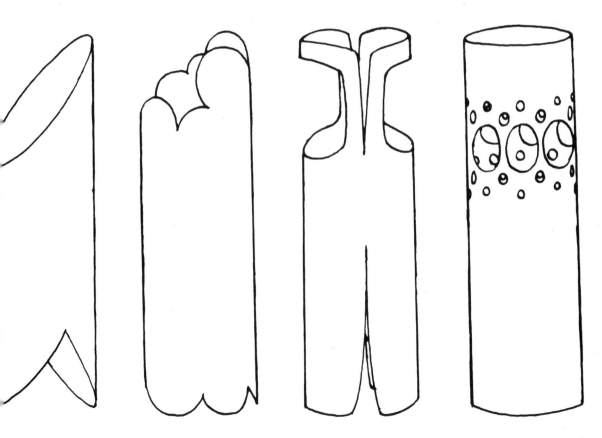

to become involved with detailed renderings of the human figure; it's quite sufficient simply to indicate the shoulder line, so that you can spend more time on the important part of the scheme, which is to create a dress design using paper and Vilene (interfacing) based on your experiments with paper tubes. The dress need not be for yourself, but for a friend, if you can find one who is willing to put up with your ideas! An important element in your thinking must be that you, as the designer, are in control; what you say goes. Ideas must not be watered down, for the outfit is not intended for normal use, but should be visualized as an exciting experiment based on creative thinking.

Now perhaps that is enough to put anyone off! This is usually the first reaction, but as soon as the experiment gets under way many interesting ideas begin to come through. Vilene (interfacing) does not behave like a normal fabric; its stiffness favours sculptured, dramatic shapes, which do help to emphasize this aspect of dress. Another quality of Vilene (interfacing) is that it will take colour and can be assembled by cutting and sticking, or by stitching. Don't go to the trouble of making patterns. It is much better to start with a basic, cylindrical shape on a person and, proceeding from that point with many fittings, create the idea by cutting and sticking. By adding accessories and decoration and thinking of the whole design from head to toe, you are now able to put many of your design ideas into a single concept. In an experimental way you have arrived at the heart of the fashion idea.

75 Designs based on experiments with cylinders. Notice how you don't need to become too involved with detailed renderings of the human figure. When working on a design sheet allow your ideas to develop slowly. Those shown here indicate the scope of the idea

9 *Sources of Inspiration*

It would be very easy to think that the factors we have been examining give us a complete picture of design. Up to a point, they offer a basic framework through which we can operate. However, they have provided a means of developing visual experience, first through awareness of the environment and second through a considerable increase in sensitivity towards line, shape, form, pattern, texture and colour.

By turning our attention towards our environment, 'seeing things we haven't noticed before,' we move towards a further stage in the design process. We are no longer happy to use stock solutions to design problems, but are beginning to realize how many alternatives there are. However, increased awareness is not, in itself, necessarily going to increase assimilated information. It is possible to receive stimulation from our immediate surroundings, but this for most people will only be for a limited period, until this source is exhausted or found incomplete. It could, eventually, become a limiting factor, which, through a lack of diversity, could bring complacency and eventually a narrow parochialism. With a wider horizon you are more likely to find different solutions to the same problem, coupled with some surprising similarities which can sometimes be quite reassuring.

When we are endeavouring to work creatively, ideas come both from ourselves and from external sources, either as initial stimulus or as detailed

Strong pattern forms.
monkey demon Dwivida,
ing mischief to mankind, an
tration to the tenth book of
garata Purana, Central India,
y nineteenth century

reference information. As far as ideas from within are concerned, we all have information from past experiences stored in our subconscious, some of it relating to events which happened a long time ago. These experiences might not be visual but might relate to smell, sound or touch. For me the smell of burning charcoal immediately brings back a flood of images relating to Africa, especially my first impressions: warm, moist air, bright light, luxuriant foliage, many shades of green, brilliantly coloured flowers, people everywhere, bright, though not garish, clothes, new shapes, new colour groupings, new patterns and sounds. In fact so many new impressions that I felt all my established visual values were being turned on end. Sounds can bring back different memories; screeching car tyres could only be Athens for me, while bustling, noisy, small cars surging along, horns blaring, is Rome. You will have memories of your own; some might suggest only atmosphere, something quite abstract, perhaps nothing more than a general suggestion of colour. It can be as simple as the sound of a stream, waves falling on a beach or rain on a window.

77 Highly patterned Brazilia moth, 24 cm (9½ inches) wide

78 Turkish banknote, of the First World War period – a rich source of pattern

79 A very formal pattern of buildings, trees and textiles. Princess with a huqqa, listening to girl musicians in a palace garden, Guler, early nineteenth century

But life is too short for us to rely completely on our own experiences; we have neither the opportunity nor the time to see and experience all the many influences which might stimulate us into developing new ideas.

Designers, painters and sculptors all respond to external stimuli; they might be the work of other designers in the same field, or the ideas of designers in quite a different sphere of activity. An architect might be influenced by a painter, or an embroiderer by a sculptor. Most designers – and this term covers everyone engaged in a visually creative activity – are curious about all things visual and make it their business to go to exhibitions, see films, books, magazines, photographs, textiles, artifacts, plant forms, insects and any other visual stimuli they can find. At one level theirs is the sheer joy of experiencing these visual delights, which in any case will provide further visual memories, while a second, more lasting way of making use of these experiences is to file a record of them for use in the future.

This can be done by collecting samples, if they are small enough and easily available, making drawings, taking photographs, or by collecting illustrations from magazines. In other words, building up a valuable library of ideas that is intensely personal; through its formation it will extend the range of the collector and will always be available for reference, or use as a stimulus when ideas are slow to form.

If you make a collection of this kind, should you limit your research to fashion and embroidery sources? This is a key question, which has been answered in part already, when we were discussing the habits of professional designers. There is a school of thought which holds that you will find enough material within your own specialist orbit, in this case fashion or embroidery, without looking anywhere else. This is quite true, especially when these subjects are considered in a global or historical context, and it is an argument which can be raised whatever your particular interest as a designer might be. Apart from criticizing a narrow specialization as slightly incestuous, there is great value in looking for visual information outside your chosen area, for nothing ever happens in isolation; idea, social background and design are all interrelated.

It is far easier to measure this relationship through the modifying influence of time. We can all identify, for example, the late nineteenth century or the 1930s through family photographs, perhaps seeing how clothes of the periods and settings evoke the atmosphere of the time. The thirties provide us with a happy hunting ground; they are sufficiently removed from today to have a nostalgic image yet they provide a first glimpse of a mature twentieth-century style which owes much to the inventions of this century. By this time cars, aeroplanes, electric power and talking pictures had begun to influence the public imagination.

Of course there were other influences, many of these being much more subtle as far as the general public were concerned. In retrospect the most important of these was the Bauhaus, a school of design which flourished in Germany between 1919 and 1933. It was founded on what was then a new concept of design training which strove to offer the student far greater freedom. Its impact on design can be judged by the fact that many creations which originated there now seem quite commonplace. The original tutors were mostly painters, who are today represented in many galleries throughout the world, while the work of its architects, either tutors or former students,

Antelope headdress, used in
s re-enacting the mythical
h of agriculture by the
ibara tribe of Mali, West
ca, 110 cm (43½ inches)

embraces some of the finest examples of twentieth-century design. Its original concept was one of an appeal to sculptors, painters and architects to find a way of returning to the crafts. In itself this was a throwback to the Arts and Crafts Movement which influenced many designers in England towards the end of the nineteenth century.

Of the many areas of study within the Bauhaus, textiles and stage costume are of immediate interest. Weaving as wall hangings, carpets, upholstery or experimental studies drew on the imagery of the twentieth century, particularly that which was first explored through painting. The results were revolutionary in a world still dominated by traditional influences, and provide a good example of how cross-fertilization of ideas can work in practice.

Contemporary embroidery owes much to the inventiveness of the weaving created in the Bauhaus. Dress or costume design has more subtle connections, although there was an immediate link with textiles we have just been discussing. The Stage Workshop endeavoured to see things in terms of the twentieth century, trying not to be prejudiced by the assumptions of earlier centuries. In the process they developed some highly original ideas for clothing the human figure based on simple geometric structures. It is interesting to compare some of more dramatic creations of Courrèges in Paris with those of Oskar Schlemmer which were designed in 1920 for the Stage Workshop.

Although the thirties was an interesting period it is not by any means the only one worth considering. We could look at the fifties or sixties in which, for example, space travel became a reality. Was it coincidence that science

81 Cars from earlier periods provide nostalgic shapes and patterns

Ornate Romanesque
~~ures around the doorway of
~~ west front of Chartres
~~hedral, France

Fairgrounds are often rich
~~exuberant decoration

84 A pair of doors full of inventive ideas, rich
pattern and an interesting break up of surface carved
about 1910 by Olowe of Ise, a Yoruba sculptor,
Nigeria, about 183 cm (72 inches) high

fiction seemed to come to life, that cars sprouted fins and in some cases false exhaust pipes, and fashion presented us with an image of the space age, the mini skirt? The nineteenth century, especially from 1850 onwards, was also a period of change. Railways spread across countries and continents, for example, leaving behind a trail of new technology, and making new uses of materials, shapes and pattern, and new space spanning structures.

Religion exerts a greater influence on our lives than we sometimes realize, whatever religion we follow. Religious beliefs have affected the way we live, our dress, and in some cases our homes, literature, art, decoration and buildings. Places of worship are often impressive in scale and rich in decorative detail. Objects of religious significance and ceremonial vestments are likely to be highly decorated or embroidered. Consider how religions have influenced one another, and how they have influenced us. What kind of impact have 'dead' religions made on our culture, for example those of Ancient Egypt?

Returning once more to the present, there are many different ways of sifting through material. Suppose we take the theme of the sea. We have the sea itself, water patterns, waves, reflecting surfaces, spray, fish, shells and marine life. While above the surface there are people as swimmers, or sailors in small boats, there are larger ships of various kinds, buoys, lighthouses and

85 Windows, whether tho of a suburban terrace, detac villa or country cottage, can form an immediate reference embroidery design

Traced studies on a page of
student's notebook

oil drilling platforms. The seashore is really bursting with information. There
are the plants and marine life which exist between high and low water, birds,
trees, grasses, butterflies, moths, harbours and the architecture of the seaside
village or town. These will all be different in whatever part of the world you
choose to look. In England mention of a seaside holiday resort often conjures
up a vision of Edwardian hotels, wrought iron railings, promenades and piers,
pavilions, amusement arcades, fish and chips and saucy postcards. So much
of this could be used as inspiration for design.

Modern technology provides alternative, less nostalgic sources of inspiration: the wires, valves, controls and chassis of elderly television sets, car engine
components, general junk in scrap metal yards and waste plastic which can
appear in most unusual forms.

Many of these suggestions seem far removed from dress or embroidery
design. So let us look a little closer at ways in which this information may be
sifted before being used. Research might develop on an intuitive level; no
doubt the most rewarding experiences will emerge in this way. Some time
ago a girl was engaged in collecting design material for future use. She started
by making some pencil drawings of the seed head of a sunflower. These
studies suggested a more three-dimensional treatment might be worth trying.
This idea emerged as a low-relief structure made from card and stiff paper
which was based on the formation and shape of the seeds. From some angles
these looked like a series of domes, suggesting those of the Romanesque
period, and this encouraged her to look at the architecture of that time and to
make further drawings, paintings and collages. She experimented with

different materials, exploring the pattern potential of the repetitive forms of Romanesque vaults and domes, while also taking a quick look at the decorative splendour of some of the domes of Byzantine churches. The trail did not end here; she soon became interested in the function of domes and the manner in which they were used to enclose space. She looked around for other structures which had a similar prime function. This route eventually led her to quite a different period of design, the nineteenth century, to the great roof spans of iron and glass used by Victorian railway builders. Once the spanning function was explored it wasn't long before she was aware of the decorative nature of the structural ironwork, which was in fact just as original in concept as the domes of the earlier period.

Through her study this girl had been looking at her material from a particular standpoint, that of pattern and decoration. By being prepared not to take everything at face value, but to search beneath the surface as it were for small details, she was able to extract information which excited her interest, while the more casual observer might not have noticed anything worth recording. Another designer might well have used the same material to arrive at quite different conclusions.

Although we have seen how drawing and painting are quite natural ways of collecting information, you may still have deep-rooted fears about using these processes in an experimental fashion, bridging a commonly held concept of what painting should be and making experimental studies with a 'design' as a final objective. You may be worried about not being able to draw and paint to a photographic likeness. To draw part of a building, or take a detail from a photograph might seem a daunting task. 'What do I look for; how do I transform it when I have found it?' This is the usual cry for help. Again, fall back on the experience you have acquired so far and simply draw, paint, make a collage or use a mixed media treatment – in fact use whatever materials seem appropriate to translate the area which is to be the subject of your study. That is quite enough as a starting point for the materials you use will bring about change, and your own handling of them will have done much more.

Try a number of studies of the same subject experimenting with slightly different materials; if you look at colour on one occasion and focus on pattern on another you will soon see how ideas may move in different directions. As all these represent intensely personal creations, like doodles on the back of an envelope, they need not move in a pre-determined direction to be an embroidery design, a dress or a particular piece of decoration, but can simply be wide-ranging experiments where it doesn't matter at all if mistakes arise. Mistakes often turn out to be most useful ideas which can later be used to advantage.

You can make extremely useful collections of photographs and other illustrative material by assembling scrapbooks with careful selection and juxtaposition of images so that subject matter takes on an entirely new meaning. These provide stimulation in those moments when new ideas seem few and far between, or when immediate, authentic information is required on some small detail.

After a shaky start – to be expected when trying something out for the first time – I find people really enjoy building up these collections. They make a useful link between earlier experiences, involving a particular element of design, and later stages when developing new ideas for dress or embroidery is the major concern.

10 *Development of an Idea*

As long as we realize ideas don't materialize in a ready made form, we won't be too disappointed. They have, on the contrary, a habit of forming slowly, taking a seemingly erratic path, and gathering substance from many sources along the way.

This notion is no longer new to you, but although we have been considering design in this way since we first looked at line, it will still come as a shock to some people that we should work in the same intuitive manner when we are working out, or creating design. No doubt somewhere at the back of our minds there lurks a puritanical notion that if we don't think the whole problem out before committing ourselves to paper, we must be cheating. Perhaps this comes from our home background or our conformist schooling, where developing free-ranging ideas and flexibility of thought, which appear very close to daydreaming, was the very antithesis of the accepted code of behaviour.

Design as applied to embroidery is usually easily accepted and understood, whether in terms of an abstract or naturalistic result. But when dress design or fashion is discussed many people can't really see how the same principles apply. To a certain extent we have seen how design most certainly does relate to dress. A particularly strong case was made when we were discussing garments based on cylindrical forms which were later made from Vilene (interfacing) and paper. We were aware of form in a sculptural context, although at that stage we were not too concerned with qualities of texture and colour. These are, of course, critical, for they virtually affect the final appearance of an outfit. Similarly, choice of hairstyle and make-up are just as vital to the total design image. Good design depends very much on attention to details, as long as they are seen within the context of the whole idea.

All these facets can be explored in a simple, direct way by using collage, a process you have already discovered, which enables you to avoid too early a commitment to a particular idea. It is a useful process at this stage, more so than drawing and painting, which can sometimes lead to a preoccupation with finished effects rather than ideas.

If you have survived the previous problems, this one is not going to present any great difficulties. Drawing a figure need not present an insurmountable problem, for there are many ways in which a basic figure shape can be made. If you look at fashion drawings covering many changes of fashion, you will notice the most successful ones are very simple in concept with what can hardly be called photographic likenesses. This is where your collection of ideas, discussed in the previous chapter, comes into use. Look through your collection of fashion photographs and current fashion magazines to find a pose which will provide a suitable prop on which to develop your design.

Bold collage in a mechani-
tint takes your idea a step
her

88 A figure drawing which shows how a pose might be interpreted in line. Rhythm is often difficult to identify, but here is one version of the main rhythm lines of the drawing. The basic nude form illustrates one form a master tracing might take

Some of the most useful are those promoting swimwear as they are the nearest thing to a nude pose. A simple pose is best, where life is expressed in terms of rhythm lines, rather than a contorted position.

One way of understanding the rhythm of the pose is to select a number of photographs, this time including models wearing dresses, coats and other garments. Using a sheet of tracing paper and a pencil, try to draw in the main rhythm lines of the fashion figure. Don't make the mistake of drawing round the outline of the figure, for the real objective is to try to discover how far lines will describe the image. After a few attempts you will be pleasantly surprised how much life there can be in these studies. In many ways you are now beginning to appreciate the selectivity required when making a figure drawing. No doubt you will see how the relationship of angle of head to shoulders or shoulder to hips and the position of feet to head are important considerations affecting the overall balance of the figure. Soon you will begin to see how shapes relate and proportions are handled, and begin to think back to your own earlier experiences in this area of design. Devote quite a lot of time and practice to working through these studies, for the most creative fashion photographers, through their own skill as designers, often select camera angles and backgrounds which clearly emphasize the whole essence of an outfit – a perceptiveness we should all try to emulate, no matter what we are making.

Returning once more to the first photograph, the girl in the swimwear, make a tracing which concentrates on the rhythm of the pose, so that all the key lines are transferred to your tracing paper. Now try a really bold move! Using the traced image and referring to the photograph, translate that image into a simple, uncluttered fashion drawing. Make sure the width of arms and legs does not become too heavy, and, if necessary, simplify their appearance by concentrating on the overall shape. Don't try to identify the muscles too much, thereby giving the figure the likeness of an Amazon, rather than that of a slender fashion model. This also applies to the extremities of the figure, feet, hands and head, which require even more careful treatment to simplify them to their most elementary form, to omit extraneous detail while preserving the elements which give character and expression to the figure as a whole. On some occasions you may feel the mouth or eyes are important as part of your design, so include them. Hair always offers tremendous decorative scope, being a mass of straight, wavy, curly or frizzy lines which can provide just the right fashionable detail to the head.

When you have completed the study on tracing paper use it as a master drawing which can later be used in many different ways. Use it, for example, as a master tracing when creating a number of different designs, or as the basis of a much larger drawing. Let us consider this last use first. Enlarging the figure to about 46 cm (18 inches) high should not present too great a problem, as long as you remember the techniques you perfected when working on the smaller master tracing. Start by going all out to capture the feel of the pose, concentrating on rhythm, shape and finally proportion. For example, in order to make the figure more elegant, make the head a little smaller in proportion to the rest of the body than it would normally be. If you look at fashion photographs you will see how many are taken from a low viewpoint which elongates the legs and makes the head appear correspondingly smaller. Don't feel you have to complete a magnificent portrait for the head;

remember you are making a symbolic figure and it is probably best to forget about any facial features other than hair.

Having established the character of the figure, you can now decide if it is to remain an outline drawing, or be cut out and placed on a coloured background which would relate to the colour of your final design. The next stage, to design an outfit onto the figure, is entirely up to you. The concept itself isn't too difficult to grasp, being reminiscent of the children's toys which have a basic figure that can be dressed in many ways. I advise you not to be too ambitious at first; a dress, skirt and blouse or casual wear would make good starters. Don't forget earlier experience with Vilene (interfacing) and paper dresses, which focused on the essence of the idea.

Now is the time to surround yourself with photographs showing current fashion trends; get a feel for current fashion colours, fabrics, weaves and

89 Fabric collage as a basis fashion design. An early stud on a large sheet of paper showing a sensitive feeling fc shape, rhythm and proportio

90 and **91** More large, bold fabric collage studies
show the possibilities of this medium

90 91

patterns. For accessories, shoes and hairstyles, soak up the feeling of the
moment. Collect as many samples of the season's fabrics as possible, noting
how manufacturers grade their patterns and fabrics to make collections. See
how unusual combinations of materials, such as plastics and fur, can set new
trends. When changes in fashion occur the retail trade is slow to respond, so
you might find it much better to get small samples from major manufacturers.
Start to consider your own ideas, not by lifting one detail from here and
another from there, but by working intuitively with your ingredients. Here,
again, your ideas collection begins to help. If you are at all unsure of yourself,
look at fashion over a number of years, and see how trends have gradually
moved in and out of favour only to reappear many years later in a slightly

different form. One method is to take a number of periods ten years apart and try to analyse the effect of rounded, soft, square or boxy shoulders, short, long or calf-length skirts, narrow or puffed sleeves, high or low necklines and narrow or full trousers on the female form.

Don't fall into the trap of using only those styles and colours which you like. Use colours or combinations of colours you wouldn't normally use and keep an open mind in just the same way as you would when making a painting, collage or pattern. Don't set out to design clothes for yourself because in-experienced designers can find this restricts their inventiveness. It is much better to adapt one of your completed designs for yourself, so getting a much more adventurous idea.

This then is the link point between earlier discussions and designing a dress, or if we look a little more widely, the whole fashion image. Having worked through a process of creating a design you now have an experience on which you can build, enabling you to launch into new ideas, some of which might be direct descendents of your original design themes. In this way your confidence will soon grow, lifting you over the difficult and fundamental hurdle between design values and traditional notions of dressmaking.

Returning once more to your small master tracing, you could use it over and over again as a basis for creating fashion images. As the scale in this instance would be smaller you will need to alter your method of handling fabric and other materials. A mixture of paper collage and painting is one method which is worth exploring. Hat, blouse, dress, skirt, or trouser shapes can easily be cut from fabric samples; if the right sample is not available, paint your idea on a piece of paper, cut it out and assemble it with the fabrics. Position these shapes carefully before you glue them down onto the figure. This should be essentially a two-dimensional solution, which could be modi-fied to accommodate, for example, knife-edge pleats. From a distance the effect can be very much like a painting, heightened with the added textural presence of the fabric. Other parts of the design, head, legs, arms and hands, could be painted as flat colour, or left as simple outlines if you think it would be more appropriate to the design. Before leaving this subject, make sure you are aware of the value of simple materials, such as different kinds of papers, or unusual fabrics which can be used to give the illusion of more exotic fabrics, jewelry, or furs.

So far we have been concentrating on design for fashion, with, some people may feel, little regard for embroidery. On the contrary; here is a point where the two areas coincide. Figures might be used in a decorative manner in embroidery, to work out ideas for dress embroidery. Detailed exploration can enable designs to be presented in an interesting visual form before you work on the finished design. To develop ideas where background and figure, or figures, are co-ordinated in a single theme can produce some surprising results. The collages were created in such a way as to allow figures and background to merge in order to create a total design. The idea itself is not new; there have been many painters and designers who have worked through this theme. Many of their designs have a particularly strong sense of period, illustrating very often how, in retrospect, we can see links between fashion and decoration as a whole. I have found a most surprising spin off from this kind of experience has been, for most people, an increased confidence in handling decoration on the figure. Perhaps it is because this process draws the emphasis away from

92 A wedding dress owing much to the design processes we have been discussing

93 A contrasting design relying on movement for maximum effect

94 and 95 Two designs exploring the effect of pattern when it is related to figures and background

the figure to another zone, that of the meeting point of body and background, thus allowing a less self-conscious design to emerge.

There are still many people who start a piece of embroidery without devoting enough time to preliminary experiment. They perhaps get an idea, or wait until they have an idea, and then act on it with almost indecent haste, to reach that golden moment when one more embroidery is under way. Time spent on experiment is never wasted. Experiment may take many forms, ranging from drawing and painting to stitchery, and use many skills. To use stitchery in an imaginative manner requires time for experiment and development; creative work just cannot be turned on like a tap. The key to the whole situation is to give yourself time to let ideas mature. Don't commit yourself to first thoughts too soon; they so often contain fundamental mistakes which cannot be eradicated during subsequent stages of development.

One of the main problems facing the embroiderer is the process of working, which is slow compared with other art forms. Concentrated work in small areas does tend to stop the designer seeing the idea as a whole. Though not too difficult to overcome for a sensitive, discriminating designer, it is hard for those who cannot help putting technique above all else.

Relaxed, expressive drawing with a soft pencil on paper can be a very useful way of starting a design by encouraging an analytical feeling for shape, colour, texture and pattern. A number of ideas can be worked over and eventually a single theme will emerge; different permutations can quickly be worked out. Later, as the idea begins to take form, other materials can come into play, in a sequence which cannot be predicted, but will be unique to each occasion. In other words, no-one can suggest either the range or order of materials which could be used, but only provide a general pattern through which an idea might form.

Ideas in embroidery occur in different ways. Absolute beginners with no experience of design are likely to fall back on clichés, and make what they feel is expected of them, rather than what they would like to do if they only had

96 A three-dimensional embroidery using patchwork, about 100 cm (39 inches) wide

the courage. They don't want to step outside the norm. Their targets are quite modest; they attempt something which is not too difficult, gravitating towards ideas which depend very strongly on technique. Someone who has thought about design might still need courage and might be confused but is less likely to accept the first idea that comes along. You could spend a lot of time desperately trying to think of something different, so original that an idea just won't materialize. I suggest you pitch your aims somewhere between the two. Don't be afraid to draw on past experiences and home background, at the same time searching for a new interpretation which would grow naturally from your own sensitivity towards those elements of design we have discussed.

Your collection of ideas, your sketchpad with experimental doodles, your alertness to your surroundings and your receptiveness to new influences all play their part. It might be just one photograph, or something you saw in the street which starts you thinking. As your ideas begin to take shape you might find yourself using further information from your collection. It might be an aerial photograph of a town or an infra-red photograph taken from a satellite of a large area of the earth's surface, a detail of a window, or any other form taken out of context as colour, shape, form, pattern, and texture. You might use your collection in other ways, taking, for example an old, faded family photograph of grandparents or relatives outside a shop or store, very conscious of being recorded for posterity. Considering the treatment of this as a design, using machine embroidery, would in itself be a translation of the original photograph. In order to judge how the idea might turn out, create the same effect by using coloured felt tip pens. These might later suggest ways of obtaining the strongest impact from the clothes, the lettering on the front of the store, or any other details which might fit into the scheme. Some areas of the design might prove unsuitable for machine embroidery; bolder treatment might be needed. For this you could use paint, paper collage or other basic materials, so that gradually the feel of the design begins to come through. Only then should you start to consider the eventual form and method of stitchery to be used in the embroidery. In any case, more design studies would still be profitable, for the first scheme probably contains enough ideas for two designs, and further selection will still be needed. You might find the original concept has changed, as you have gradually begun to discover the real potential of your original source material.

More experiments might move your ideas still further away from your original concept and redirect your thoughts to other reference material in your resource collection. This could be pattern in, for example, Islamic painting which has a strong two-dimensional pattern quality, or the super-realism of some painters of the 1970s. Gradually you will begin to drift towards materials and processes which will give form to your thinking, through collecting and experimenting with materials and stitches. Try to capture the full textural splendour of the design which makes embroidery so rich when compared with any other fine art medium.

One example can not hope to sum up the full scope of embroidery, but it does illustrate the way in which an idea can take shape and how this relates to basic design values. None of us knows the full extent of embroidery and there are no doubt very many ideas and uses which haven't been discovered so far. This brings us back to the need for continual experiment, and a constant awareness of design amongst embroiderers.

97 A richly embroidered slipper

98 A highly decorative, intuitive hanging, about 122 cm (48 inches) high

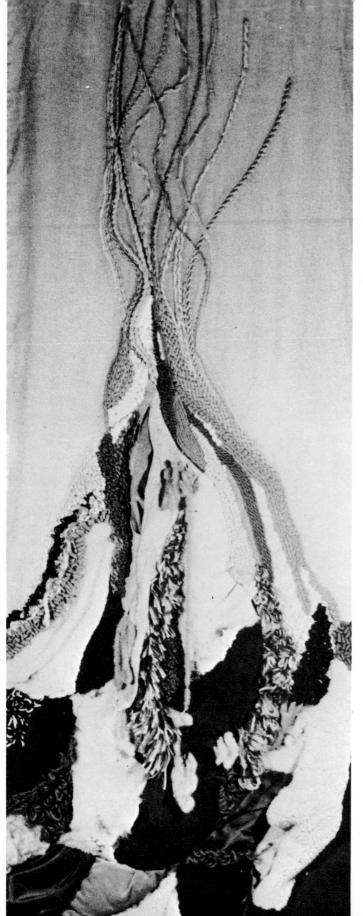

99 A hanging exploiting different surfaces and materials, about 244 cm (96 inches) high

11 *Criticism*

How do we know whether our creations are good or bad? How much of what we create is affected by personal preference? How are personal preferences formed? These questions are often asked by people who have been trying to make stimulating, original designs. In so doing they will have been probing, exploring new avenues in very much the way we considered earlier, and yet they still have nagging doubts which cloud their achievement. That these questions have been asked, and that these doubts exist are healthy pointers towards a critical, thoughtful outlook. If you encounter smugness, implying the design is above criticism because it was completed by an expert, then there is real cause for alarm.

Answers to these questions can never be straightforward, for they depend on many things. There are enormous differences between individuals, and even differences within a family. To expect clear-cut answers would be quite wrong. We all share common experiences but as individuals we all value freedom of choice, and like to express this freedom through our own personalities. However, we all desire some form of acceptance from our peers and tend to take notice of prevailing ideas and fashions. We like to be seen to accept new ideas. This does not always involve discrimination. Some people maintain that a fashionable look is all that matters, while others take a different approach, considering the expression of individuality to be more important. This latter group are unlikely to ignore fashionable trends, for we cannot help but soak up influences from our surroundings. Sometimes fashion can help a whole generation assert its independence. It is interesting to observe art students, who should through their own inclination and training be forward-looking individuals. Their creative freedom appears to be a matter of tuning in to the latest fashionable trends, in a desire to project the right impression to other members of the group. Often they seem to want to overthrow last year's ideals with the greatest possible speed, in order to be first in scenting and hastily adopting new ideas as they appear. So eventually, at a superficial level at least, they all appear to have the same ideals; it is only as they mature that true individuality occurs.

Happily, with more mature students, this frantic search for recognition doesn't seem to occur and there tends to be much more honesty of purpose. While they do not necessarily follow every fad of fashion, they combine open-mindedness, sensitivity, breadth of vision and attention to detail, with a unique ingredient, their own personality. A situation which the younger person, through inexperience, dare not risk, for fear of stepping outside those values dictated by the group. The sternest critics of imaginative ideas are those who never had the opportunity or inclination to rise above values, which became set while they were in their teens. While it is convenient to subscribe wholeheartedly to this dogma, how many of us could honestly say we are free from every form of prejudice?

What does this imply as far as fashion and embroidery are concerned? Surely we can't profess to be open-minded in design and think in traditional terms when considering techniques? Some people do attempt to do this. Instead of talking about techniques, they substitute 'being practical'. So we have people who would say they are all for design but we must be practical. This implies that a new idea can't be tried out because the process won't stand it. It is often much nearer the mark to say that the speaker is not prepared to look at the overall problem, the design and execution of an idea, from an original viewpoint, or to acknowledge that there is more than one way of approaching a problem and this could be influenced by materials and processes. To change techniques or allow them to become too fluid is too much for the traditionalists, for it erodes those values which have been built on a single platform of technique. To defend this viewpoint is a natural defensive action.

Nonetheless, imaginative designers have always defended the preservation of traditional processes and values, while keeping their eyes open for new approaches to broaden the spectrum of design.

Leaving aside the influence of the personality and outlook of the individual, effective criticism can be practised by using simple questions. These can be combined in different permutations to apply to many forms of design, whether simple or complex. Some of these will consider shape, form, texture, pattern and colour, as appropriate. Don't always think of them in isolation, but combine two or more areas as required. Let us consider a design which could be a complete fashion image containing accessories, make-up, hairstyle and garments, or an embroidery. If colour was its strongest characteristic we could begin by asking a few questions relating to colour.

> How has colour been used?
>
> Why has it been used in this way?
>
> Has this objective materialized?
>
> How have colour relationships been handled?
>
> Have harmonies/discords worked?
>
> Have tone values been considered?
>
> Could they be lighter/darker?
>
> How would this change the design?
>
> Has colour been emphasized or broken down through pattern or texture?

These questions are by no means the only ones which could be asked, though they provide a general pattern. Some of the answers might appear to be similar; this doesn't matter for they are really probes which enable you to obtain a much clearer understanding of the design. They should help to clear away the mist of instant comment and replace it by a discriminating vision.

As you can see, the questions themselves are not complex. In fact they are so simple that many people are inclined to overlook them, or fear that such basic thoughts might be considered ignorant. So they resort to a more acceptable stance, asking what they hope are more erudite questions. This approach is doomed to failure for it is only by asking a series of simple questions that we are able to build a complete criticism.

This proposition alone isn't going to enable you to overcome your apprehension of being able to evaluate your own or other people's work. Whether or not you use the term taste, its implications of superiority persist, though expressed in different ways. Another word which we could use in its place is discrimination although even this can suggest an attribute of superiority, awe-inspiring to the average individual. The only way in which discrimination can be acquired is through experience. This is a gradual process, which cannot be speeded up. Experience alone is not enough. It needs to be channelled in the right direction; many people have a lot of unrealized experience which has somehow to be unlocked, or recalled, sifted and collated if it is to be of any use at all. One of the aims of this book has been to start you moving along this road, encouraging you to become aware of the visual world. By realizing the interdependence of one culture, one artform, on another you will see how we can start by looking at embroidery or fashion and end up by examining design as a whole.

This aspect was reinforced for me when I listened to a talk given by a costume maker who has made many period costumes for films, television, opera and the stage. In describing his methods of research he talked of his need to step inside a period, to soak up its influences through studying its social history by looking at wills which often mentioned articles of clothing, by examining drawings, paintings and architecture so that gradually he was in a position to create garments which were technically and aesthetically correct in cut, handling and decoration. There is a lot to learn from the breadth of his research and the awareness of period which grew from it. Rather than saying, 'This garment was worn,' he asked the more fundamental question, 'Why was it worn?' If we do our research properly we are going to become different people; little by little we will be able to compare cultures, to compare one period within a culture to another, and to weigh one form against another. We will in fact be exercising discrimination.

This is the difference between the person who is willing to discriminate and the ordinary man or woman who is willing to pass judgement on anything they see. Why do we get so upset when Mrs. X says she doesn't like a dress, or thinks some embroidery is awful? Why do we tend to throw all our ideas overboard when someone refuses to listen to our point of view? We are hurt; we like reassurance. I'm sure you won't find the conductor of an orchestra trying to meet a potential audience half way, by watering down, or popularizing the music he is about to conduct. His attitude would be that if you listen without prejudice you will gradually be able to appreciate some small portion of the work. If you were to hear it again you would understand more, and given time would probably enjoy it more fully, or at least be able to evaluate its content before deciding whether or not you like it.

There are many people who will postulate the merits or demerits of a particular design; they might make impressive noises, mutter long, obscure words or phrases, and even frighten the designer by making profound interpretations of his or her modest intentions. What do we do with these people? Either leave them alone, or, better still, test them with a few simple questions, to see if they are uttering fashionable phrases or expressing sincere thoughts, before listening to what they have to say, or allowing them to sail by to blow their hot air somewhere else.

This is not meant to imply arrogance on our part, but that we should listen carefully to see if any of the points which have been made are relevant, and through this try to differentiate between critics. Sometimes, quite by chance, a very simple but pertinent observation can be made by someone with no previous experience of design. The speaker might be totally unaware of the value of the comment, but that simple, unsophisticated remark could clear up or illuminate a problem which has been worrying a designer for some time.

With clothes fashionable trends play a considerable role in the formation of a design, yet it is surprising how some designs which are fashionable at the moment of their inception, or are very much in tune with their period, rely on design values which prove to have a lasting quality which enables them to transcend time. They may move out of favour for a few years, their impact deadened by sheer familiarity, only to be rediscovered by a later generation. This so often happens, although it can be difficult with a new design to distinguish between fashionable 'tat' and emerging new ideas. It's often much easier to say, 'I told you so,' than to make firm statements at the time. I wonder how many innovations in design have been greeted with derision by the professional critics, only later to be recognized as most important advances? Consider also the number of designers who were the darlings of their age, who later faded into total obscurity.

I suppose, therefore, there is some measure of hope for us all.

Further reading

Ballo, Guido, *The Critical Eye: A New Approach to Art Appreciation*, Heinemann, London, and Putnam, New York, 1969

Brochmann, *Odd, Good or Bad Design?*, Studio Vista, London, and Van Nostrand Reinhold, New York, 1970

Garland, Madge, *The Changing Form of Fashion*, Dent, London, and Praeger, New York, 1970

Landmarks of the World's Art (a series of ten volumes), Hamlyn, London, 1967

Laver, James, *Modesty in Dress*, Heinemann, London, and Houghton Mifflin, New York, 1969

Munsell, Albert H., *A Grammar of Color*, Van Nostrand Reinhold, New York, 1969

Naylor, Gillian, *The Bauhaus*, Studio Vista, London, and Dutton, New York, 1969

Ostwald, Wilhelm, *The Color Primer*, Van Nostrand Reinhold, New York, 1969

Sloane, Patricia, *Colour: Basic Principles and New Directions*, Studio Vista, London, and Van Nostrand Reinhold, New York, 1968

Index

Figures in italics refer to illustration numbers

Adinkra cloth   40, *41, 42*
Adornment   37
Architectural design   *86*
Artistic ability   14
Assemblage   60, 65
Awareness, visual   14, *15*

Balance   32
Bauhaus   73, 74
Bead embroidery   *53, 54, 97*
Beauty   28, 29
Block printing   *35, 41, 42*

Calabash   *34,* 40
Centre of interest   20, 56
Chroma   55
Collage, paper   *29, 40, 60, 62, 66, 67, 87*
   fabric   60, *63,* 65, *89, 90, 91*
Collections   83, 88
Colour   92
   additive   54
   application   54
   complementary   54, 56
   prismatic   53
   proportion   56
   temperature   55
Concept   68
Confidence   11, 12
Contrasts   15, 31
Crafts, traditional   9
Creativity   71, 78
Cylinders   *12,* 68, 69

Decoration   39, 59, 69

Designers   14, 73
Design for embroidery   28, 87
Discrimination   93
Drawing   25, 27, *32,* 77, 78, 86
   figure   *24,* 79, 81, 87, 88
   natural forms   *5, 19, 21*

Education   10, 11
Embroidery   39, 50, 74, 87, 88, 92
Environment   7, 14, 58, 71, 72
Erté   (*see* Fashion Drawing)
Experience   22, 58, 78

Fabrics   83
Fabric design   19
Fashion   *1,* 39, 42, 65, 91, 92
   colour   51
   drawing   *22,* 82, 83
   ideas   91, 92
   trends   82, 83, 84, 91, 94
Flowers   62
Form   32

Great Exhibition   10

Hue   55

Images, negative   (*see* Positive and Negative)
Indian painting   76, 79
Interfacing   19, 70, 82

Jewelry   *38,* 65–8, *71, 72*

Katsura Rikyū   36
Knitting   *50,* 48, 62

Line, straight   18, 56
   curved   19, 20, 23
Looking   23, 24
   (*see also* Visual Awareness)

Machine embroidery   22, 55, 50
Mass   30
Memory, texture from   44

Negative   9, 16, 33
   (*see also* Line, Shape, Image)
Newton, Isaac   53, 54
Notebooks   78

Pastel crayons   5, 23
Patchwork   96
Pattern   37, 94, 97
   formal   12, 40
   free   40
   random   41
   in nature   37, 44, 45
   sources   39, 77, 78, 79, 81
Photography   25, 81
Plastics   46, 62, 67
Pleating   19, 42
Poiret, Paul   24
   (*see also* Drawing)
Positive   33
Poster paint   21, 22

Random effects   22
   (*see also* Pattern)

Religion   58, 76
Rhythm   19, 81
Rubbings   44, 47

Scale   15, 35, 37, 41, 68
Sculpture, African   4, 80, 82
   fairground   84
   Romanesque   83
Sensitivity   22, 56
Shape, awareness of   30
   creation of   68
   in embroidery   28
   in fashion   28, 29
   geometric   33
Space   21, 24, 25, 34, 35
Squares   33, 34
Stripes   19
Surfaces   37, 44, 49, 56, 99
Surroundings   23, 37, 43
Symmetry   65, 69

Technique   13, 68, 92
Template   20, 62
Texture   (*see* Memory, Rubbings
      and Surfaces)
   trees   46
Tone   55, 57
Traditional design   34, 35, 38, 39

Volume   30

Weaving   41, 50, 62, 74